Colored People Time

COLORED PEOPLE TIME

A Case for (Casual) Rebellion

MANNY FIDEL

ONE WORLD
NEW YORK

One World
An imprint of Random House
A division of Penguin Random House LLC
1745 Broadway, New York, NY 10019
oneworldlit.com
randomhousebooks.com

Hardcover ISBN 978-0-593-73066-9
Ebook ISBN 978-0-593-73067-6

Printed in the United States of America

1st Printing

First Edition

BOOK TEAM: Production editor: Cara DuBois • Managing editor: Rebecca
Berlant • Production manager: Mark Maguire • Copy editor: Jenna Dolan •
Proofreaders: Liz Carbonell, David Goehring, Dan Janeck

Book design by Kevin Quach

The authorized representative in the EU for product safety and compliance
is Penguin Random House Ireland, Morrison Chambers, 32 Nassau Street,
Dublin D02 YH68, Ireland. https://eu-contact.penguin.ie

To my newborn baby girl

*A minimum of comfort is necessary
for the practice of virtue.*

—PATRICE LUMUMBA

✳ Contents ✳

Colored People Time

1
FROM TIME

It's dark. And when I say "it's dark," I mean it's dark everywhere. And anywhere. Perpetually and all-encompassing. Nothing exists yet. But "nothing" exists. "Existing" doesn't even exist, but the absence of existing does. It is emptiness, if something that doesn't exist can be empty. The most brutal, or gentlest, of realities, depending on your perspective. But your perspective doesn't exist yet. And then, in a split second: everything. A giant explosion? A big bang. Galaxies are now zooming through an infantile "universe," whatever that is. These galaxies float and expand in incomprehensible ways. They seem random but are also the exact shape they need to be. This is infinity.

It's awesome. Not in the way that the NBA playoffs are awesome, but in the literal sense of the word. Awe-inspiring. Only, there's no one to inspire just yet. There are no mailmen or teachers or police officers or politicians or pundits. There are no children, no teenagers, and no adults, no elders. There are no feelings, no emotions, no conflicts, no wrongdoings, no good deeds. There are no good times or bad times. There is no justice, and no peace.

Just time. From time.

Stardust is flowing through the clouds on adolescent planets like Mountain Dew through the veins of a *Call of Duty* enthusiast in 2009 who will try not to call me the N-word after losing in an online match. He will fail, but these planets, in their apparent mission to sustain life, will not. At least one planet will succeed and set forth a derivative series of events that could be described as beautiful or regrettable, depending on your perspective, which, for the record, will exist soon, relatively speaking.

The planet Earth, our home, does not begin in a calm manner. We start off with molten rock. Seas of lava crash into one another like patrons at an overrated bar on the Lower East Side of Manhattan. This is Earth's least habitable form. As extreme as the start of the universe. A smaller planet lunges into Earth and ejects continent-size pieces of rock into space. These massive boulders come together and form the moon, which sways Earth's oceans a billion years after the curtains fall on their teenage magma phase. And then, the first sign of life: microbial organisms, or "microbes." They just sit there and writhe in the dirt. Pulsating and throbbing without a single thought in their minds. Pushing ahead for reasons unknown to them. I'm envious. Eventually, they become mushrooms and plants and vegetables and, at some point, fish.

Narratively speaking, the fish flop out of the water and grow legs. Running around the world, reproducing, they create a web of different hideous creatures born with the mission to keep remaking themselves. Different climates affect these creatures and change them, making them bigger and even uglier. Some of them grow wings and fly away, untethered to the drama on the ground. The dinosaurs arrive and rule the earth for 165 million years. They are wiped out by an asteroid that is approximately six miles long. The rock came from the depths of the universe that, in the meantime, has been endlessly unfurling, stretching, and expanding. As the universe is infinite, there are infinite planets going through these similar growing pains. I wonder if any of the infinite options will end up as tedious as ours.

On Earth, we're back to chaos. Millions of animals are obliterated in an instant, and millions more starve to death due to the extreme conditions caused by the asteroid. Annihilation for 75 percent of living species. The remaining 25 percent, though, bounce back. They're not just the stepfathers of life; they're the fathers who stepped up. The first primates begin to evolve over time. First gorillas, and then chimps. The ancestors of humans diverge from the chimp lineage. One such creature from this new lineage lives in what will become Ethiopia. For some reason, millions of years later, scientists will name her Lucy. ("Luam" or "Lemlem" would have been a more geographically apt option, but I digress.) Lucy's nieces and nephews migrate across the globe and become *Homo sapiens*. Depending on where these *Homo sapiens* settle, their skin color begins to change. The less the sun rules your land, the lighter your skin becomes.

I must pause here for a moment of silence.

The earth's most intellectually advanced creatures are about to become tragically stupid.

Homo sapiens' brain function isn't where it is today, but they manage to use tools and make jewelry and create villages. They have families and maintain relationships. After some time, they develop empires and send explorers around the world, partly out of curiosity but mostly to procure resources for their growing populations. When these civilizations interact with one another, we return to chaos. They are different, so they must fight. War, rape, theft, famine. Slavery. For thousands of years. There are winners, and there are losers. Famously, the winners dictate what becomes history, even as I recite it to you now. The Persians stretch their influence from Iran to Egypt. The Han dynasty lasts four hundred years. The Umayyad Caliphate rules over four million square miles of land. The Ottomans conquer three different continents. The British Empire rules over a quarter of the world.

It is this last empire that facilitates much of the slave trade in the Atlantic Ocean. Africans are ripped from their villages to be enslaved for the proliferation of agricultural resources. In the year 1619, a handful of them are the first of their kind to set foot on American soil. They are trafficked to Virginia by a British vessel called the *White Lion*. Much like the *Mayflower*, which will land at Plymouth Rock a year later, the *White Lion* will go down in history as an incredibly consequential ship. The Africans arrive in Hampton, Virginia, and are sold to Governor George Yeardley, who keeps them in Jamestown. Before his arrival there, a harsh winter had recently hit. By the end of it, a fraction of the people survived. The other residents either starved to death or were killed by Native Americans. Things got so bad that Jamestown residents started to eat each other, which was especially harrowing for them as white gentrifiers of sorts; this was a few hundred years before quinoa was popularized as a side dish. Then, help sailed in from England in the form of Yeardley, a man tasked with rehabbing the American locale like in a demented episode of *Kitchen Nightmares*. He is successful, but as with many of the country's early triumphs, he had support in the form of the forced labor of enslaved Africans.

That is, albeit simplified, the story of the *White Lion,* which is, surprisingly, not the name of a shady aphrodisiac behind the counter at your local convenience store. The *White Lion* is actually one of many overly self-important names for slave ships in that era. Others include *Expectation, Deliverance,* and *Independence*—hilariously not the subtitles for Michael Bay's *Transformers* films. Almost every terrible thing that has ever happened to Black people in America can be traced back to these ships and their eye roll–inducing names. There is some pain in knowing that the names of the ships that trafficked human beings for profit were likely created by the dorkiest guys imaginable. I can't help but picture a rosy-cheeked Londoner dipping his feathered quill pen in ink and being proud of himself after writing down a name like "The Brilliant Hog."

But I've digressed again.

The enslaved Africans are forced to toil in America for hundreds of years, operating as the gears that move the country forward into industrialization. Some of the greatest atrocities in the history of mankind are committed against them.

In time, the patch of grass the Africans were taken to is titled the United States of America, a name that strikes fear into the hearts of the natives who lived there first. And while the land is modernized with the blood and sweat of natives and Africans, those united states go through an identity crisis. Should America be a racist country that allows slavery or a racist country that doesn't? This painfully laborious inquiry becomes the foundation for how life is defined for the descendants of the previously mentioned Africans. Those descendants' pursuit of equity is perilous, and they are threatened at every turn. It is during this moment of national rumination that a notable but historically overlooked human is born on a plantation in South Carolina.

Robert Smalls is born to a Black mother and a white father on the McKee family plantation. His mother, Lydia, is worried that his fair skin will blind him to the full extent of the atrocities of slavery, as lighter-skinned slaves are treated with less aggression on average, and the McKee family does favor him. After Robert grows a bit, Lydia makes him work in the fields with the other enslaved people, so he can witness their abuse at the whipping post. This will radicalize him. Years later, Robert is rented out to work at the Charleston ports, where he learns the waterways like the back of his hand. While on the docks, he meets his wife, Hannah, with whom he has two children. All this in the midst of a Civil War. Confederate boats in Charleston can't sail too far north; otherwise, they'd run into the Union naval blockade and be fired upon. However, the same ships forming that blockade are also accepting runaway slaves. If a slave can make it to the blockade, they can become free.

It's dark, but the moon is illuminating the Port of Charleston. Despite breaking free from Earth billions of years prior, the moon is about to learn a lesson in escape. Smalls and a group of enslaved men take command of a slave ship called the *Planter* while its two white captains are distracted elsewhere. They are probably pontificating about Black-on-Black crime. Smalls and his group sail out of the docks and toward the Union blockade, picking up Smalls's wife and children on the way. Smalls is able to make it through several Confederate checkpoints not only because he memorized the signals he used to see his white captains give, but also because he wears a captain's hat and, thanks to being mixed race in the dark of night, kind of just looks like a white guy. Once past the checkpoints and approaching the blockade, Smalls orders his ragtag crew to ditch the Confederate flag and don a white flag of surrender. They finally reach the blockade, and it is, according to at least one historical account, party time.

"When they discovered that we would not fire on them, there was a rush of contrabands out on [the ship's] deck, some dancing, some singing, whistling, jumping," writes historian James McPherson, quoting an eyewitness on the scene. Robert Smalls had successfully freed himself, his family, and the enslaved crew of the *Planter* and fooled Confederate soldiers to do so.

In comparison with the birth of the stars, Earth's swaths of magma, the microbes, the dinosaurs, and empires—and contrary to how slavery and civil rights are framed in the American educational curriculum, which would have you believe that Martin Luther King, Jr., shook hands with a

KKK member and ended racism in the 1960s—
Robert Smalls's burning desire to be free wasn't
all that long ago. Smalls died relatively recently—
in 1915. His niece Amelia Boynton Robinson—
a civil rights activist who became famous when
someone took a photo of her being beaten by police during the 1965 march from Selma to Mont-
gomery, on the infamous "Bloody Sunday"—died
in 2015. Her son Bruce Carver Boynton was also a
famous civil rights activist and helped spark the
concept of the Freedom Riders, groups of activists who rode buses into segregated states to protest inequality. He died in 2020. The wounds of
hatred and inequality are fresh and in living color,
and the weapons that created them are still being
sharpened today.

Around the world, other cultures also suffered
the effects of racist ideologies. The British deliberately exacerbated Indian famines for profit, and
colonialism by European states is responsible for
the slowed development of African nations over
the course of hundreds of years. The devastation
wrought on the rest of the world eventually forced
millions of people to pursue the so-called Ameri-

can dream, which ironically began with a pilgrim-age to a land housing people who would hate them. My mom and dad found themselves in the middle of a war for independence in Eritrea, a country on the Horn of Africa. That war, which ended in the early 1990s, could have happened only in the wake of Italian dictator Benito Mussolini's invasion of Ethiopia in 1935, which was made possible by Italian occupation of the region in the late 1880s. For *that,* Italy has to thank the Berlin Conference of 1884, a meeting of European nations that regulated colonialism in Africa.

People of color often get to play this deranged version of connect-the-dots when looking at their family histories. My parents, who fled Eritrea but first met in Sudan, decided they wanted a better life for their growing family and applied to come to the United States under asylum laws. After they were accepted, their trip was delayed because Saddam Hussein invaded Kuwait, causing international tensions. I was almost born in Sudan, but thanks to our travel to America being greenlit once again, I popped out in Dallas, Texas, which is responsible for my support of the Dallas Cowboys, which is a tree that has not yet yielded one single fruit.

There are millions of stories similar to ours, and injustice will produce millions more.

Indeed, as globalization persists and resources wane, conflict will thrive. The building blocks of these conflicts will be cemented together by classism, and the solutions to these conflicts will primarily benefit whichever groups of humans are on the top rung of the ladder by then. As the planet deteriorates, one such solution will be to leave altogether. Even as I write this, the world's most bored billionaires are racing to see who can escape Earth's atmosphere most efficiently. We will spread human culture beyond Earth and into the Milky Way. There are going to be slurs and stereotypes on Mars. Next to a nice Martian suburb will exist a daunting and strategically placed highway separating it from the neighborhood where the three people with modest incomes who made it off Earth will live. On Jupiter's moon Ganymede will exist a gas station whose security cameras activate only when certain people walk in. At a nightclub on Neptune, some patrons will wait longer for a drink than others. The reason for this, historically speaking, will be because, tens of thousands of years ago, a group of people thought *Damn, it's kind of hot,* and walked somewhere that was a little cooler. They left the patch of grass on which they were born and went somewhere with slightly different-colored patches of grass, and their skin lost color. They departed from home—just like their descendants will tens of thousands of years later.

When it comes time for the latter departure, the return to the stars, one can only hope those privileged enough to leave the ailing Earth behind will grasp the cruel irony in their doing so. Tens of billions of years of seemingly accidental delib-erations of the cosmos led to the perfect planet. The existence of Earth, a planet that can sustain life, is a mathematical error. Even so—even with the knowledge that, statistically, we shouldn't be here—we will have ruined it in a relatively short amount of time. And as we spread the worst parts of our nature across the galaxy, I hope the pioneers of this excursion will come to terms with how trivial the root cause of these troubles was: One day, man traversed the world to reach a colder climate and his complexion changed. From time, it was the beginning of the end.

2

TICKING TIME BOMB

Sometimes, teachers let students lobby for where they would sit in the classroom. Whenever I got that opportunity, the back of the room was the goal. There, I'd be out of Mrs. Robinson's line of sight and could more freely doodle on my desk or sneak in some crucial minutes on my Game Boy Color. In the back of the room and away from authority's gaze, I could also engage with my crush, Destiny, as she always managed to be in the last row of desks. Once, I ripped out pages from the "Igneous Rocks" section of our science book and cut out the diamonds as a gift to her. "Oh . . . um, thanks!" She loved it. The back of the class was also an opportunity. One's trip to the pencil sharpener doubled as a catwalk, a lane for kids to show off the new clothes their parents had bought with Kohl's Cash, and for me to exhibit one of the many Ohio State hoodies I owned, also from Kohl's. It was a dream back there.

In the fourth grade, the clouds parted and the sun shone down on Highland Elementary School in Columbus, Ohio—and I successfully got a seat in the very back of the classroom. But my placement immediately backfired. Back there, with everyone facing away from me and toward the front of the class, I couldn't display my hoodie that read OHIO STATE BIG TEN CHAMPIONS, instead of the one I'd worn the day before reading OHIO STATE CONFERENCE CHAMPIONS. My ears also suffered every time a kid with a booger creeping out of his nose came by to sharpen his pencil in the rusty metal pencil sharpener. I wonder if the screech of that decades-old tool in desperate need of lubrication contributed to the tinnitus I'd develop later in life.

One morning, the school principal walked into my classroom and whispered something in my teacher's ear. It might have been easier to hear if I hadn't banished myself to what was essentially the stadium nosebleed section of the classroom. I needed a distraction from the waft of pencil shavings that invaded my personal space, and the drama unfolding at the front of the class did the

trick. Both adults—who, in my head, were in their
fifties, but who were probably actually in their
twenties—scurried out of the room, leaving the
gaggle of fourth graders alone to crack jokes about
what we thought happened. Did a fifth grader
clog a bathroom toilet? Did a crack user make
their way onto school grounds again?

While we pondered this, the intercom system
began calling kids to the front office because their
parents had arrived to pick them up. I didn't know
why everyone was going home, but I was envious.
Mrs. Robinson rolled in a boxy TV on one of those
wheeled AV carts and turned on the news without
saying anything. I think that was the first time in
my life I felt disturbed. I didn't know exactly what
was happening onscreen, but I knew it was wrong.
After school—I was one of the few kids whose parents understood that Columbus, Ohio, was not a
target of international terrorism and was thus not
picked up in the middle of the school day—I walked
home with my little sister. It was a short and quiet
walk. At home, we found my mom glued to the TV
while folding laundry. We asked her what happened in New York City, and in her thick accent,

she said it was "very bad." Months later, my dad
tried to make it make sense for me.

"A long time ago, a group of people lived on a
river," he began with his perpetually wise de-
meanor. "Suddenly, strangers arrived and sucked
the river dry. The people who lived there could no
longer live healthily, and it made them very upset.
Some of them became filled with rage and hurt innocent people."

My dad was doing his best to simplify the U.S.
military's aggressive presence in the Middle East,
to speak about it in a way a nine-year-old would
understand. It wasn't a defense of what happened;
he was simply giving me the Kidz Bop version of
events. Unfortunately, in my youth and innocence,
I took his story literally and told everyone at
school that 9/11 happened because the Americans
were sucking up rivers in the Arab world. The
kids were confused.

"Why would they do that?"

"We have our own rivers."

"Okay, well, there's a river behind my grand-
ma's house."

One day the following year, I even enlightened

a teacher with this reasoning while I was waiting for her to finish grading my homework. Knowing nothing of the nuanced geopolitical dynamics at play, I unwittingly simplified the conflict even further. "There would be no 9/11 if we just left people alone." This interaction was proof that the Department of Homeland Security hadn't been created yet, because no SWAT-style operation came to whisk me away before I could finish my sentence.

My teacher sneered at me with a face that said *I knew it*. She had just encountered directly what white suburbanites only whispered about while picking up their morning edition of *The Columbus Dispatch* from the driveway: supposed evidence of terrorist sympathizers inside the United States. From then on, I felt something change in our relationship. It took me years to recognize this shift: Despite my being barely old enough to read *The Columbus Dispatch,* let alone comprehend its content, I wasn't given the benefit of the doubt and was being treated differently in class. She couldn't give me lower grades—my parents were extremely present in my studies and would catch anything remotely resembling a discrepancy—but she was short with me. She stopped calling on me when I raised my hand, stopped letting me use the bathroom without a scoff. She was cold and unforgiving. Why? The unspoken yet visible disdain that shaped her interactions with me became the focus of my after-school thoughts too, and I started to learn how to read between the lines with people who appeared friendly but who perhaps harbored more sinister feelings.

In the grand scheme of things, 9/11's impact on me was relatively trivial. The attack took thousands of lives, and the main victims of post-9/11 bigotry were Muslim and Sikh Americans, who faced hate crimes and saw their faith being framed as the antithesis of American Christian values. And as if Hollywood writing weren't already reductively imperialist, seemingly every film and TV show villain for the next decade would be an Arab Muslim. I grew up Catholic, but to the unknowing eye, Americans, brandishing a monocle made out of gold-plated American ignorance, regarded my East African family and me as vaguely "Muslim," and that was enough for people to call me "raghead," "Ay-rab," "sand nigger," "hijacker," and more, mostly at school. Outside school, I rarely felt like a minority, as I spent my childhood either playing video games with my cousins or hanging out with kids in Columbus's Eritrean community. Sure, there were a few sour interactions with white teens from the neighborhood, but the xenophobia I faced was mostly confined to school grounds.

Facing bigotry at a young age forces people of color into analytical thinking before they should ever be burdened by it. As time went on, I started wondering where my classmates had learned their colorful insults. I thought about their older siblings and their parents. The internet was still relatively young then, but maybe they'd seen the words on some forum or in a comments section. Were these kids just products of their environment, or had they made an active decision to be mean? And if they were just parroting others, did that even matter? Did it make it better? It didn't change all that much, from my point of view. These invasive contemplations provided me, and scores of other Black and brown kids, a regrettably early path to understanding nuance. To look at a situation and understand its context, as a child. To think, in the face of a hurtful encounter, that there was something more under the surface of it. Far too soon in life, I and others like me developed a sixth sense that many people don't ever have to develop. How did we get to this moment?

Growing up as a Black or brown kid requires a level of hyperawareness, and at a time when we should be chiefly concerned with whether the main characters in *Power Rangers* will defeat the latest alien sludge monster in the next episode. (They will.) In the Western world, we have to navigate societies that see us as others, while also appealing to the sensibilities of the systems ruling those societies. This was a burden on me, and the breezy innocence that defined much of my adolescence was replaced in part by a pinching sense of consciousness. In this way, critical thinking wasn't just an academic skill learned over the course of a boring semester in middle or high school. It became a tool for walking through a world riddled with implicit bias.

From too early an age, people of color are

tasked with accurately assessing certain social cues and confronting the iffy narratives espoused by their white peers—peers who usually approach the world with an inherent trust in its institutions. I often think about how some of my Black and brown friends come off to others as weary, skeptical, jaded, or cold and wonder if these first impressions would be different had they been given the benevolence of a carefree childhood. Instead, during that time, we all weathered at least a few existential fights. Before I even knew how to talk to girls, I had to determine whether a criticism leveled at me was merely constructive or subtly prejudiced.

In the havoc of the school day, I occasionally fought back. Once, I was riding home after hours and hours of seventh-grade orientation activities. Our bus would sometimes pick kids up from a nearby school. Like water and oil, our two factions did not mix well, and a few minutes after the kids from the other school got situated on the bus, it was on.

"They have terrorists at Westmoor?" one white kid joked from the front of the bus, gesturing toward me. He had bleached-blond hair and a face like a tiny, expensive dog.

I made the necessary calculations: I could either ignore what he'd said, which would be embarrassing, or defend myself, which would probably also be embarrassing. I decided that if it was going to be embarrassing either way, I might as well hit back.

"You look like your parents are siblings," I yapped, falling well short of a confident delivery. I got a couple of laughs but didn't quite shift the mood.

All the kids whipped their heads back to the front.

"Someone check him for a bomb!" the kid retorted.

The laughter was thunderous—the kind of laughter that isn't really about the joke, but the target of it. You know the kind: where it doesn't matter what's being said, but whom it's being said to.

At this point, I stood up for a final attack. "I don't have a bomb, but I made your mom explode last night."

Lackluster. It didn't make enough sense to the other kids' newly pubescent brains, and this was clear from the near-total silence that followed. To be honest, I don't even know if *I* knew what it meant, but I understood that it was supposed to be insulting. Had it not been for the bus's loud diesel engine as we lurched along the pothole-riddled streets of Columbus, you could have heard a pin drop. In this instance, it might as well have been the pin of a grenade.

My opponent stood up. He was wearing an oversized Marc Ecko T-shirt and a single diamond stud in his left ear. He took a deep breath, smirking at me in my OHIO STATE ATHLETICS shirt. "This is what you sound like," he said, followed by a spattering of gibberish and tongue clicks that were supposed to be a foreign language. It was a cheap shot, but the delivery was buoyed by an admittedly funny physical performance, as he waved his arms and hands about.

The children on the bus went up and down, up and down, rolling in their seats, snickering like little rats. This was before Michelle Obama "radicalized" the school lunch system, providing kids with healthier meals—and fruits and vegetables were hard to come by. But if there *were* tomatoes around the schools back then, they would have been thrown at me and onto my proverbial stage.

Two decades later, I still find myself making excuses for my subpar performance in what I believed at the time to be a valiant fight against racism. In stand-up comedy, punching up is more honorable than punching down. It requires more thought and effort and, most important, risk. Additionally, my unchosen audience represented a narrow demographic, and middle schoolers are eager to hear a more deprecative brand of jokes.

The drama on the school bus that day was just one of a million examples of racist confrontations from that time in America, and this racism caused me to be much more careful when I spoke. If I wanted to express something, I ran through the full spectrum of possible reactions, rehearsing my responses accordingly. To say something as simple as "I like Disney movies" required me to first play a game of chess in my head. What if the kid I'm talking to says, "I'll bet your favorite one is *Aladdin*." Should I laugh it off? Return the hostility? The burden of early-onset critical thinking plagued my childhood, and it wasn't until college that the noise began to clear.

The Ohio State University. A metropolis of a campus, a city in its own right. And like most cities in the state, its population was overwhelmingly white. Many students were liberal, but the outspoken conservative student presence was more apparent—from "the Oval," a park and gathering place where evangelical student organizations chastised female students for wearing shorts on a hot day; to my political science class, where a student claimed that President Obama's radical liberal policies forbade police officers from using someone's race while describing a suspect. (Of course, this wasn't true, and of course, race is often the first descriptor given.)

There was a ton of stuff to do on campus. I'd lounge at a coffee shop that tripled as a record and comic book shop, and I practically lived at one of the worst campus bars on earth, a place called Charlie Bear that featured comically sticky floors and blared Top 40 music, even when the sun was still up. Yet as much time as I spent pursuing the one league-required girl on my intramural soccer team or obsessing over the football team's upcoming matchup, I spent just as much time endlessly mulling over the racist encounters I experienced on campus. The most notable occurred one night during my sophomore year, while I was walking home from the campus Waffle House. Trayvon Martin's murder was heavy on the minds of those of us who cared beyond the optics of caring. I would soon learn it was still on the minds of drunken frat bros too, when someone among a group of them hanging out on their porch shouted in my direction, "We got a Trayvon over here!"

The other boys, who exhibited all the diversity of a six-pack of Bud Light, erupted with laughter, flashed their teeth, and threw their necks back, gnashing and gnawing. The air was filled with chewing tobacco–flavored saliva and the contents of a can of Pabst Blue Ribbon that had spilled onto the porch in what was gratefully the only casualty of the encounter.

"How am I a 'Trayvon'?" I asked. "I'm not even wearing a hoodie." Not that wearing a hoodie calls for harassment, but I was trying to connect the dots. Was it because I was walking home, like Trayvon had been?

"It's just a joke, dude," one of the frat boys barked.

"What's the joke?"

The six-pack, so to speak, was confused, but over the course of a few more puzzled looks, things started to come together for me. Unlike the one I'd dished out on the school bus years earlier, his "joke" didn't need to make sense. There was no humor or wit involved; the topicality was enough. Yes, the boys were laughing in a physical sense, but their laughs acted more as a signal of approval. Rather than genuinely finding the comment funny, they were simply telegraphing a political view. They wanted to make light of Trayvon Martin's death because they had been led to believe not only that his murder was justified, but also that sensitive liberals were stupid for thinking it wasn't. There was no use in pointing out why the comment was racist, because the racism and, specifically, the conservatism were the point. It's racist to see a Black guy and say, "Look, it's Trayvon!" but it's also deeply political, the speaker unable or unwilling to shift in his stance. How, or why, would I combat that? Standing there, newly enlightened, I turned and kept walking.

This revelation brought me an unexpected sense of relief. Until then, I believed that ignoring a prejudiced encounter was a cop-out and that I should be doing more to combat the transgressor. Afterward, I learned to consider the lack of humanity in these interactions and disregard them accordingly. For me, shrugging off such an encounter is less about conflict avoidance and more about understanding how absurd racism is at its core. I decided not to expend any effort on people who were too far gone in their political echo chamber. It's not that every racist is a lost cause; it's just that finding out whether they are, after a one-off encounter, is a waste of time. I might have learned this later than my peers who are also people of color, but engaging with people who can't be bothered to think deeply can never be fruitful: You're already working harder than they are by default. And you can apply this logic to every racist: Their purpose isn't to make sense or provide insight; it's to agitate their target, sometimes to underscore their racist beliefs and sometimes just for fun.

I'm not arguing that people should let racism slide off them the way some unfazed superhero immune to bullet penetration might. In fact, channeling anger in these moments can be productive and rewarding for many people.

Instead, I think about what it would mean for kids of color to grow up in a world where their worth wasn't questioned, a world where their anger didn't need to be channeled because the injustice that sparked it didn't exist. Adolescence lived in bliss.

When it comes to the weight of such encounters, I won't hold that weight forever. As cliché as it is, every bigoted encounter taught me something valuable about myself and about other people. I can't go back in time and give my younger self the autopilot feature that should come with adolescence, but what I can do is lean into what I've gained. Sometimes that manifests as a more nuanced sense of humor; sometimes it's just a story to tell at a party. The world hasn't changed as much as I'd like it to, but I have.

Since reaching adulthood, I've felt an urge to give myself some remote version of the blitheness I often lacked in childhood. I'm making up for lost time.

3
HOW TO GROW A LEMON TREE

I lost my mind a little during the first few months of the Covid-19 pandemic. The highs and lows of delusion. I barely slept, tweeting into ungodly hours of the night, and I was often awake until my West Coast friends, three hours behind me, submitted their own disconcerting 3 A.M. posts. Their late-night thoughts—like "what if we kissed in Wuhan, China" and "Tulsi Gabbard can get it"—were my cue to finally log off and go to sleep for two or three hours, until it was time to start my work-from-home day.

At the time, I was churning out depressing content as part of my media job's "Covid response team," which consisted of making graphics and videos about how many people had died each day, with a soundtrack of seemingly constant sirens just outside my window. In that early stretch of the pandemic, I didn't know what about Covid-19 was true, what wasn't, how the virus spread, or how to keep myself safe, beyond making sure I—

at the time, a late-twenties, physically active, healthy man—kept myself away from others so as not to pass along an asymptomatic case of Covid to someone for whom it would be much worse. So, I stayed in my apartment all day. At one point, a friend of mine used his allowance of outdoor time to jog to my apartment and catch up with me on my stoop. I sat at the top, and he stood at the bottom, which we both supposed was at least the six feet in distance required by the CDC. When I offered him a beer, an example of how little we knew about the disease arose: We both thought that the millisecond during which both our hands were on the bottle simultaneously could be *just* enough of a spreader event that it could end up killing four grandmas in Queens. We decided to keep them alive.

It didn't occur to me how lost I was in space and time until my dear friend and then-roommate Emmanuel texted me: "Is everything okay over there lol." You see, earlier that day, I had posted on Instagram a step-by-step guide to make a milk and honey bath because I read that Cleopatra often cleansed in this manner. It included images of me taking the bath, along with fun-fact pop-ups and diagrams reminiscent of a doodled-in middle school textbook. In my defense, I think it was fairly informative content, and more to the point, my skin was positively glowing after the experiment, so it was a success. But it was the selfies taken from a bathtub of milk that justifiably prompted concern from Emmanuel. He has always had incredible foresight, and that spring, at the beginning of the pandemic, he had temporarily moved to D.C. to be with his then-girlfriend. The relocation made sense, but my being alone in our large, old two-bedroom apartment was a catalyst for my state of disarray. I wouldn't call it a mental breakdown, but it was maybe a mental departure of sorts.

Due to Emmanuel's move, I was tasked with receiving his packages, including a very special one. He told me he bought a lemon tree, thinking he'd be there to take care of it, and asked if I could take on that responsibility. I couldn't say no even if I'd wanted to: I had literally nothing to do. Consider that in that time I spent alone, I once glimpsed my feather duster out of the corner of my eye and, thinking it was an animal that had broken in, felt a fleeting sense of excitement that another living being was in my proximity. I was happy to take on the challenge of caring for the lemon tree as something, anything, to do with my time.

The tree arrived in a long, rectangular box that I had to carry up three flights of stairs while it leaked dirt out of all its gaps. My new dependent and I made it to the apartment in one piece, but no matter how carefully I opened the package, the dirt continued to spill, and I made quite a mess. After a ten-minute struggle, the tree was finally revealed to me. For some reason, I imagined it would arrive already bearing fruit. Instead, it was just a skinny stem with branches that sported a handful of leaves. It reminded me of myself in middle school.

I stood it upright and placed it inside a big pot Emmanuel had set up before he left. After that, I thought my job was pretty much done. Water it every now and then, and it will grow some lemons, right? I had such a remedial grasp of plant care. Wanting to present like a responsible person, I always had at least a few plants of my own around my various New York City apartments throughout the years, but I specifically chose ones that even a monkey could take care of: monsteras, money trees, and the like. But this tree was different. It was the rare dating app match that you actually care about, the one you get a haircut and maybe a new shirt for. Never mind the "why not" variety of Tinder swipes—this was the real deal. I called Emmanuel for instructions.

Step 1: Place the tree strategically.

Apparently, lemon trees need about eight hours of sunlight per day. Eight hours is a little much. How many hours of sunlight do humans get on average? I'm not even sure I total a full hour per day. In New York, you often have to leave the house to go searching for direct sunlight, and this tree needed eight hours? All right.

I placed the tree in front of a south-facing window in our living room. But putting the tree right next to the window meant it was always silhouetted by the light, and I could never get a good look at it unless I got really close. It was therefore easy to miss when leaves were yellowing or when the soil was too dry. The silhouette of the tree always looked good, though, hiding its flaws. Even if the tree posted nude selfies in a milk and honey bath, the sun's light would shield it from any concerned, head-scratching viewers.

During that early phase of the pandemic, when friends would ask how I was doing, I'd respond with what I thought was true: "I'm pretty good, considering" or "Things are chill." It's not that I was in a truly bad way—there are much worse mental health symptoms than bizarre social media activity—but I realized I was presenting a silhouette of myself to my friends. I texted Emmanuel at one point: "I think I have a leg up on everyone dealing with quarantine because I'm always in my room anyway lmao." It's a text that seems carefree, but that "lmao" was doing Olympic-level heavy lifting. In reality, I was upset. Frustrated at the state of things. Yellowing at the sides like the leaves of the lemon tree. Oh right, the tree.

Step 2: Feed the lemon tree.

As it turns out, water is not some magical ingredient that can sustain life on its own. A given organism, like a lemon tree, also needs food, especially when that organism is confined to a tight indoor area. Lemon trees specifically need nitrogen, magnesium, and iron, important components for plant cell growth, respiration, and division. Emmanuel had already bought plant food with these ingredients in it, and for the first few months, I fed the tree like it was my child. I even worried about whether it was hungry, perhaps overfeeding it at times. I realized the power and responsibility I had, that there was a life in my hands. If I failed to properly tend to this thing, it would cease to exist. I felt like a god, albeit one who had to set a timer to remember when to water and feed his subordinates. Growing the tree became a true regimen. I planned my day around it. Wake up. Tree. Eat. Work. Tree. Shower. Tree. The pattern ruled my life, giving me something to do in a city where there was no longer anything to do. I fed that tree so many times, and I loved every moment I had with it.

My own eating habits changed around then. I found out just how much food and drink I put away during the various social activities that were no longer available to me. Hors d'oeuvres at a media party, fruit cups sold in Prospect Park, fried pickles at a sports bar, not to mention the two high-calorie cocktails I used to require an hour before the aforementioned media party, helping me muster the mental strength to nod in agreement with an editor in chief when he emphasized, for the second time in an evening, the importance of journalism. Social snacking opportunities had vanished, and eight pounds of my body weight went with them. It kind of blew my mind that approximately eight pounds of my body weight existed solely because I hung out. Sans these social gatherings, I found that I ate about two meals a day. Pretty much everything else I used to consume, I realized, was technically in excess. I began to eat an amount of food that simply sustained me until the next meal, and I became leaner as a result.

I wondered what would happen to the lemon tree if I gave it more fertilizer than it needed, as if it were going out a few times a week. Would the lemons it eventually bore be plumper, like my cheeks used to be?

Just as my cheeks used to fatten up in a gluttonous winter, the lemon tree's buds started to bloom into flowers. A lemon flower is the epitome of beauty. Four or five white petals act as an amphitheater for a special performance. The petals feel like silk. Onstage, a dozen graceful performers in white robes and yellow headdresses dance around a woman in a green gown. They bow in reverence to the woman. They want to please her, but they can't. Something else must be able to reach her. The dance emits a smell that lights up the room.

Step 3: Pollinate the lemon tree.

For my entire life, I knew that bees "buzzed," but I never once thought about why. They're just crazy little guys, I guess. They get a little nervous or something, so they vibrate, literally increasing the vibes. *Maybe bees buzzing is like humans talking about the weather,* I must have thought. From the research I did to tend to this tree, I learned that the buzzing of bees is far more consequential. Actually, the world would not exist if bees didn't buzz. Entire ecosystems, biomes, even, function only because bees are doing the labor of pollinating plants and crops. And the way they pollinate is by alighting on a flower and buzzing their bodies so vigorously that tons of pollen comes out of the anthers. They then fly around to other parts of the plant, pollinating it, allowing it to bear fruit or seeds. Meanwhile, the bees eat the pollen or feed it to their babies. It's a mutually beneficial relationship that makes me think about how ridiculous the concept of life is. There are trillions, quadrillions, of microscopic interactions happening that have no purpose other than to make sure they keep happening.

When it came time for me to pollinate the lemon tree, one of these interactions faced an obstacle: I had no bees to my name. If this tree were out in the wild, its pollination would have happened automatically. Instead, the tree was stuck in my apartment, just like me.

"How do I pollinate a tree without any bees," I asked Emmanuel over the phone.

"By hand."

What?

"It's not as hard as it sounds."

I learned that parts of the flower must come into sensual contact with each other to grow a lemon. The dance between the men in the robes and the woman in the gown.

The lights seemed to dim. The room was silent except for the wind caressing the windowpanes. I looked at the flower, nervous, but it invited me to calm down. I lifted the flower and, with the tip of my index finger, slowly rubbed its filaments in a circular motion. It felt like ages. I kept rubbing, twirling. Finally, the filaments gave way and enough of their pollen burst onto my finger. I then looked at the center of the flower, which housed a small nub at the top of a phallic structure. I took the filaments' pollen and caressed the nub softly. Its sticky string of secretion stretched from the nub to my finger when I pulled my finger away. I locked eyes with the nub. You could cut the tension with a knife. The flower's petals and filaments drooped a bit with exhaustion. The tree was pollinated, and I needed a cigarette.

Step 4: Prune the lemon tree as necessary.

The lemon tree was the first living organism I had taken care of that needed this level of care. The only pets I'd ever had were two parakeets my parents bought for me and my siblings. They'd earlier implied that if we got good grades, we'd get a dog—which was what my sister really wanted. After we were presented with the birds instead, my dad imparted some of his classic wisdom: "You can't even take care of your rooms. How can you take care of a dog?" We named the birds Snowflake and Stripes, based on their appearance, and because they were in a cage, they were low-effort responsibilities. One day during the summer, I felt bad that they were caged up all the time, and I took them downstairs to our basement to let them out. I was probably ten or eleven, and

I thought that they'd hop out of the cage, stretch a bit, maybe have a chat, and then waltz back inside. Instead, they broke my heart. Upon my opening the cage, the birds hightailed it straight for a closed window at the top of one wall. It immediately dawned on me that these guys hated being in a cage and wanted to go out into the world and fly around and be birds. I was distraught. With the help of my siblings, I put them back into the cage. But my compromise to Snowflake and Stripes was that I would sometimes keep their cage outside on our back porch so that they could get some fresh air. During one of these porch vacations, a stray cat ripped the cage open and took Snowflake. We found his body in an alley a block away. He wasn't torn to shreds, so my older brother determined that he had died from shock. Stripes spent the rest of his life visibly shaken from the ordeal.

I couldn't let this happen to the lemon tree.

Pollination happens in nature, but what about pruning? When a branch doesn't produce flowers (and thus, fruit), an online guide told me, it can be cut to improve airflow and maintain the general aesthetics of the plant. I imagined the lemon tree's leaves and petals scattered around the living room like Snowflake's feathers in that alley behind our house. It didn't make sense to me, a man with the least green thumb in the world, that I should cut off parts of a tree to keep it healthy. *Damn. We're just cutting off the ugly parts?* Removing unsightly twigs from a tree felt purposeless, except to improve its silhouette. Maybe the twigs and the frayed wood were unnecessary, but they were still part of the tree. Bars, restaurants, friends, libraries, and theaters are all technically nonessential elements of existence. But when those things were cut off in early 2020, did our lives get better? It isn't fair. The tree should be able to keep its twigs. Then again, the pandemic had caused me to lose eight pounds. Was that a tragedy or just some pruning?

Step 5: Snap out of it.

I pruned the tree and tossed the twigs out the window, into the backyard of the apartment building, which was private for the garden unit but had been left vacant when the twin residents moved away at the onset of the pandemic. They, like so many others, decided that New York City just wasn't worth the trouble if it was closed down. I briefly thought about heading back to Ohio, but in the haze of my solitary confinement, I understood that I was living in a two-bedroom apartment for half the price. It was just me and my best friend's lemon tree, both alive and well despite being a bit tattered.

After some time, little lemon bulbs appeared on the branches. They looked like raindrops anticipating their fall to the ground. Being as dumb as hell, I didn't know that lemons start off green before they turn yellow, and I wondered if Emmanuel had accidentally ordered a lime tree. I welcomed the potential mistake because one of my pandemic hobbies was pretending I was an amateur mixologist shaking cocktails for a humbly-sized Instagram audience, and I could have easily incorporated limes into my nightly routine of just barely changing the recipe for a margarita that I found online, passing it off as a totally original creation.

As the number of lemons grew, the city began

to tiptoe back to normality. Bars were open again, but only their outdoor sections. Friend groups began seeing each other if they could test negative for Covid beforehand. The lemons on the tree hit a growth spurt. A light appeared at the end of the tunnel. I had been trapped with my own thoughts, and the thoughts of millions of people on social media experiencing their own taste of mania, but now I felt myself progressively calming down. And as I did, the lemons grew. They weren't yellow yet, but they were plump.

Months passed. Stores opened. People returned. Emmanuel moved back in. New York City wasn't bustling, but it was getting there. When Covid hit, the city that never sleeps had become the city that boasts about staying out late but that, in reality, Irish-exits a party around 11:30 P.M. By the time the lemons were the size of golf balls, New York City had once again become the city that could stay up past 1 A.M. Our daily routines were finally injected with some variety the way my arm was injected with the Johnson & Johnson vaccine I opted for in order to hit the streets sooner than my friends who'd taken vaccines with longer wait times. Instead of doing three things a day, I upgraded to four or five. Slowly but surely, we crept back toward the usual.

Funnily, during this time, content that lambasted "the usual" proliferated online. Tweets, posts, TikToks, and YouTube videos about "hustling" and "grinding" exploded. Gary Vee, Andrew Tate, and other guys whose names also sound like the names of villains in 1990s Nintendo beat-'em-up games told millions of people that they were trapped in a loop of mundane irrelevancies and that they were all programmed to be programmed. We're just little ants following whoever's in front of us because that's all we know how to do. The only way to break out of this mold, the hustlers and grinders said, was to stray from the ordinary and understand that "routine" is a trap you need to free yourself from. Why? To make millions of dollars, of course. How? They'll tell you if you subscribe and donate to their platform. Surely it never made any sense. The world relies on procedure. If bees decided to diversify their revenue streams (or whatever) and stop pollinating flowers, the entire world would suffer.

And being a part of a system isn't nearly as shameful as exploiting the angst of young people for profit. How could I, of all people, not understand the value of a program while deep in the fog of quarantine?

By fall, the lemons were fat, yellow, and ready for harvest. As much as I found that I needed the tree in the early summer, I didn't hesitate for one second to give the reins of care back to Emmanuel. I was surprised by this. It felt like the tree and I were two strangers who were trapped in a mine somewhere in Appalachia for an extended period that proved to be traumatic but that also became a source of bonding and fellowship. After being rescued, we acknowledged to each other how crazy the whole thing was, patted each other on the shoulder, and then said, "All right . . . well, have a good one."

Emmanuel picked the lemons—there was only ever a handful, enough to make about four glasses of lemonade. I had imagined baskets of lemons, jars of homemade lemonade, lemon pastries, a bounty. I sat there for a few days, wondering if I needed to make a forced metaphor about how the journey was more important than the destination. Indeed, the act of caring for the tree provided me with purpose in a pointless world. But four lemonades?

I made and drank one. *A bit tart,* I thought.

4
THE SUNRISE UBER

Lights pass me in a kind of rhythm, timed almost to the beat of a song I can't hear. The glow from outside reveals beads of water streaming down the glass and colliding into other droplets. The droplets disappear until the next light passes. I feel a physical force, a thrust, propelling me forward. There's a river below, and I feel cold. I hear the roar of an engine. The streaks of water turn, horizontal now. I'm gliding just above the ground. Euphoric transcendence . . . until we hit a pothole.

I fell asleep in the Uber on my way home, again. I was coming from a warehouse party in Bushwick, where it took until five in the morning for me to realize that it was time to go and that the remaining stragglers weren't worth approaching. Not an insult per se; they probably felt the same about me. My friends had left at least two hours prior, but I decided to stick around. When they left, the party was still lively. We had enjoyed ourselves, moving from room to room, watching disco lights scurry away like pigeons do when you walk by. When my friends departed—for a bodega, to grab some sustenance before bed—I was eager to continue waltzing around the warehouse. An hour of weird, almost unintelligible interactions went by, and I found myself standing in a secluded courtyard within the building. Despite being outside, I could still feel the intense pulse of house and techno music. I watched a group of four pass a cigarette around. They were dressed in boxy, all-black outfits that looked like some kind of uniform. I thought about engaging them, but something was off. They weren't exactly arguing, but they were upset, waving their hands about. I went back inside and into one of the rooms designated for dancing. It was tiny, but the heavy haze from a fog machine made it feel infinite. I could hear and feel people, but I couldn't see them. They slipped by me, back and forth, grazing my sides. I became claustrophobic and exited. Back in the main room, I found what the party's promoters were calling the "bar." It was just a couple of folding tables aligned together and a "bartender" who had simply given up, allowing anyone to make their own drinks. I turned around and made a visual pass of the party. It was a little bleak. Sparsely filled with people moving like zombies. All right, that was my cue.

In the years since that party—it was in 2017, when I was still relatively new to New York City—I've thought about what kept me there so long. I'm someone who's often late to arrive at events, but as it turns out, you can be late to leave too. There's certainly cultural significance to staying out late, a kind of societal currency. The longer you're able to stay out and party, the more fun you appear to be. Cool, fashionable, interesting. People want you around. Of course, there are many, *many* exceptions to this—I know some folks whose partying habits should concern them—but, generally, that's the concept. We see it in the mystery surrounding Jay Gatsby, which is seemingly intensified by his ability to throw a good rager. And when screenwriters write expository scenes for a character who is well liked by the people in their world, it's not uncommon to see said character buzzing through the night's many attractions.

Tom Cruise's character in *Vanilla Sky* and Leonardo DiCaprio's character in *The Wolf of Wall Street* could have briefly befriended each other on a night out, pontificating to an audience of five or six fascinated people. They're not doing it for the attention, like someone jumping into a pool at a frat party. They're out there because the night requires it.

I don't think a desire to be cool—or, at least, to appear to be cool—is what keeps me out, though. It isn't FOMO, the "fear of missing out," either. I skip parties and events all the time and am very content to either hear about them later or not hear about them at all. No, what keeps me out is something that happens while the night is developing, long after I've mustered the strength to leave my apartment and wade into the dark.

I have a kind of dependency. An ardent desire for interaction for the sake of it and for the interactions that branch out from there. It's an impossible curiosity, the kind that kills the cat. It's an addiction to seeing how certain dynamics play out, whether they be platonic, romantic, or otherwise. I have a craving, maybe driven by libations, to extract all possible purpose in a given environment, within reason. I want to bond with this new friend. I want to flirt with this girl. I want to introduce myself to the seemingly uniformed vagabonds in the backyard of this warehouse party. As the night goes on and on, a weird allure takes control of me, a compulsion to exploit all available encounters. And even within those encounters, I want to seek out all available conversation. When some, or even most, of the group I'm out with is ready to head home, I'm doing behind-the-scenes negotiations with other, potentially more socially inclined people to see what's next on the night's agenda—its later chapters and even its epilogue. I have an itch to uncover the unscripted narratives of the evening, to witness characters flourishing or failing. The excitement of such moments seems to linger in me long after they pass. They give me a high. But like most highs, subsequent ones might not be as strong as the last. And so, I'm always chasing. The journey doesn't end until there are no more stories to be told.

This need for contact has rightfully become a joke: I'm the friend who, upon seeing the lights come on at the club and hearing the DJ tell everyone to go home, asks, "What's next?" I'm not unique. After-parties exist for a reason. But I've long been reckoning with what precisely I gain by my insistence that things should keep going.

Naturally, this fixation often leads to my being in cabs or Ubers at a very late hour or at the very beginning of the sun's rise. During these "sunrise Ubers," the orange to blue to black gradient in the sky is nature's signal to me that I have yet again overindulged. At this point, it feels like this indicator is the only reason the sun even comes up anymore. I'm reminded of when my parents told me as a child that I could play outside, but only until the streetlights came on. By that time, the sun had already begun to set, and it was probably a good idea to go inside, but officially, I could stay out until the lights came on. A couple of decades later, inside a sunrise Uber, my new curfew was when the streetlights turned *off*.

The sunrise Uber is my opportunity to reflect on whatever circumstance I've just departed from. I am literally leaving the night behind, and for at least twenty minutes, I can fondly reminisce about the evening, or criticize it, or litigate and relitigate it. The ride is a buffer, a liminal space in time. It's an elevator or a tunnel. It's a moment to consider whether the night was worth the effort. When the first streaks of sunlight strike the sky, I'm reset by the literal break of day. My pursuit of the night's many spontaneities is suddenly distilled into something routine: the actual Earth revolving around the sun and spinning in such a way that it makes the sun appear over the horizon outside of the Uber window. As the car drifts onto Atlantic Avenue, my thoughts wander.

I suppose that planets spinning around a star according to their own specific schedule was the first-ever instance of a routine. When a celestial object like a star or a planet is large enough, it warps the space around it and draws other objects in. Imagine a trampoline with marbles scattered over it. The marbles just sit there. But if you put a basketball in the center of the trampoline, the slope it creates will cause the marbles to inch closer to it. Replace the basketball with a bowling ball, and the marbles will really be moving. That's what's happening with stars, planets, and moons, I think.

Celestial objects can have this influence on space and time, and so, I think, can concepts here on Earth. The dark night has a massive weight. It draws me in like I'm a speeding meteor. The pull is so strong that NASA sees me as a threat and puts together a crack team of scientists and astronauts to intercept my impending collision with Earth. They fly into space to stop me, but another celestial body appears spontaneously behind me. It's my friend who's smirking at the corner of a bar, drinking a martini and telling everyone about her promotion at work. NASA's team of astronauts are confused but relieved. They begin their journey back home. What's this? A dwarf planet has come into existence beyond the horizon, and I am drawn to it. This time it's a DJ who is annoyed that people keep requesting songs. He tells me that people don't understand the difference between a real, intentional DJ set and the duties of a more pedestrian DJ, the kind hired to play a prom or a birthday party. He's right, and I nod reassuringly, saying that I would never do something like request a song from a DJ—even though I previously have. I certainly won't again. As a former pizza delivery boy, I am familiar with performing a thankless (read: tipless) job. I feel solidarity with this DJ.

A gaseous planet appears. I am vibrating toward it. It is a bartender who is upset that he has to work during the FIFA World Cup game the next morning. Normally, he wouldn't mind, but the World Cup is in Qatar, which means he'll have to open the bar at 4 A.M. for the 5 A.M. matches. He's taking his frustration out on random things in the bar; he throws a remote control and breaks a glass. Good thing I'm the only one here. After a while, he cools down and apologizes for his behavior and says that no customer deserves that. "It's all good," I say. He tells me this is normally a bar where Arsenal fans come to watch their matches and asks if I have a favorite Premier League team. I don't, but I tell him my girlfriend is from England and her family is from Manchester and that she's a die-hard Manchester City fan. He seems to have gotten an idea. He digs around somewhere under the bar and pops back up with an old Manchester City jersey that someone left there years ago. He says he washed it and tells me to give it to my girlfriend.

I am pulled toward a nebula. It's a woman at a club in Bushwick who is claiming that she's an escort for a star in the NBA. I interrogate the premise. I mean no offense to her, but I imagine that if this particular athlete, a multimillionaire with a big ego, had an escort, she wouldn't look like a barista from a college town in Indiana. I'm making an assumption, but I'm pretty confident here. After some lines of questioning, she concedes that she is not the NBA star's private escort but that she would like to be.

After more exchanges, I'm in another sunrise Uber, reviewing how I got there. I have again forced myself into an evening's poem for longer than I should have. But I need to exist in those moments, not necessarily because they are interesting or exciting, but because they are available. And they are infinite. Peeking out the window, I see the sky that is becoming blue is endless, and because it's so vast, it feels like a mirror for the countless happenings occurring beneath it. I think about the countless things that happened before I was born, the finite number of things that will happen while I am alive, and the limitless number of things that will happen after I die. Are these outings valuable because they're important to me? Or are they trivial because if all of them are important, then none of them is important? "What if"—the driving philosophy of my night—often becomes "What the hell?" when I think about my night in more than a cursory way. Luckily, I never have to dig too deep: The drive is never long enough to give the rumination any justice.

"Right here is good."

I get out. The birds are chirping. That's usually a welcome auditory experience, but after a sunrise Uber, the birds' morning song is a disturbing signal that I shouldn't be just now going to sleep. By now, most of my friends have been asleep for five to seven hours.

On my way up the stairs of my apartment building, I think about how good those extra hours of sleep would have been for me, but I also think about what it would mean to skip the moments that seem to nourish me just as crucially as sleep. I think about my friend at the bar, the frustrated DJ, the angry bartender, and the alleged escort. Those episodes will air regardless of whether I'm physically present for them. But insofar as we are all the centers of our respective worlds, those things don't actually happen unless I'm there to perceive them. It's not FOMO at all, in the end; it's more fundamental than that. I suppose that I am saving lives. When I leave a restaurant or an office or a subway car, everyone inside freezes in time until my brain needs to grasp at them again. When I return from a vacation abroad, everyone in Italy or England or France ceases to exist in a physical manner until I return. Likewise, when a friend of mine leaves the coffee shop we met at, I, from their perspective, transition to some celestial realm, not truly existing until they see me again.

I enter my apartment content that my dependency on the night has allowed the partygoers and bar patrons and passersby to exist in the first place, and now I know I must continue going out and staying out so that they are brought back into existence, even momentarily. It wouldn't be fair to them otherwise. Our lives are contingent on clocks, countdowns we can't always see. My time is limited, and there's no better use of it than to be a timekeeper for someone else. I slide into bed and put my sleep mask on. It means that I only barely see the sunlight. After a long night out and a brief morning, it's dark again.

5

THE
PROCRASTINATION
REPARATION

When the Zulu warriors of South Africa learned that British forces wanted to capture their territories, they must have been pretty bummed. After all, they were equipped mostly with shields and spears, and they had heard of the weapons the British used—metallic beasts that ejected death with a force so fast it couldn't be seen. The warriors knew that when the rosy-cheeked British troops raised their arms, that invisible power would strike them before it even made a sound. The idea of resistance was silly, but the Zulu king felt otherwise, so they prepared to fight.

One specific Zulu regiment, which, for the purposes of this story, we'll call Bravo Team, was stationed some miles away from the impending battle, sequestered at the mountain peak of Isandlwana. As a unit, they were steadfast in their goal to defeat the British forces. But individually, they quivered. Barefoot, they marched for miles, and during the long journey, they thought about what the battle would yield for their destinies. Would they die? If so, how? Mutilation? Decapitation? By bullet or by knife? Would they need to drop their spears and come to their comrades' aid? Some of them might draw their final breaths defending their friends. Some of them could be tasked with flanking the enemy in a suicide mission intended to divert attention. Meanwhile, explosions of fire and dirt would riddle the hills. But maybe Bravo Team, in the face of ostensible doom, would start to see the momentum shift. Maybe whatever atrocities they faced in battle would be worth it. A pile of their bodies could be used as a backdrop in front of which their king could announce the defeat of the British, and that would be an honor. Maybe they'd die by the time of the delivery of the victory speech, but back in their hometowns and villages, they would become heroes, legends whose achievements were sung in annual celebrations. The thought of this legacy was more than enough motivation to fuel them. They marched across the final stretch to the battlefield, ready for the inferno.

But they were late as hell. And Alpha Team, the comrades they had so nobly been tasked with supporting, had not only already won the battle but had left the area entirely. Bravo Team's morale was completely deflated. They slowly made their way across the grounds, walking around or over the scores of British soldiers who were woefully unprepared for the might of the Zulu warriors. Minus Bravo Team.

The firm confines of punctuality robbed them of their glory—but to be fair, they were alive.

The Zulus obviously didn't mean to be late. Things happen. Maybe they got a bit lost along the way, scratching their heads while trying to figure out which way was west. *Where does the sun set, anyway?* Maybe they broke out into song during a break and needed to get to the good part before continuing their march into battle. "Just wait till you hear the chorus," one Bravo Team warrior must have said to another. Or maybe they wanted to be a little late, fashionably so.

I never intend to be late to a party, but when I am, I like to imagine everyone there twiddling their thumbs, waiting for me to enter and revitalize a mood that isn't necessarily dull but could be better. This categorically never happens, but I like to imagine it does.

It's okay to be late to parties, sometimes. But I am no Zulu warrior, and neither are you.

There are plenty of events with rigid start times—say, a dinner or a movie. In cases like these, one's lateness can actually hinder other people's enjoyment. If you're late to dinner at a restaurant, your friends have to wait for you to order, or worse, they can't even be seated until you get there. Being late to an intimate drink with a friend means your friend will sit for some time alone, thinking about how to repel the leering man at the bar who is deliberating a pickup strategy he learned on YouTube. Not the worst thing in the world, but your friend could have used this time for something more productive, or even something not very productive but in the comfort of their own home.

But being late doesn't just affect how long someone waits for you. Your delayed arrival could be a disruption for someone delivering a speech or presentation, or it could impact your own personal enrichment, limiting you from fully immersing yourself in whatever activity you had planned. And famously, if you're a Zulu battalion that shows up late to a battle, you might be screwing over your comrades who depended on your punctuality to, well, stay alive.

In the Western world, the only thing worse than being late is being late repeatedly. You become known for messing up plans, and people start to think of you differently. Your constant tardiness is a sign to others that you don't respect their time or commitments, and when you are late, you strain your relationships with them while gaining a reputation for egocentrism.

Our society is organized around punctuality. No one has ever said, "Let's meet at the park," without also suggesting *when* you should do so or invited a friend to a movie without having a showtime in mind. The negative consequences of our being late make sense, then. But as with the battalion that was late to the battle but found out they'd won anyway, there is something to be gained from reassessing our attitudes toward lateness. And if I'm being honest, a certain demographic stands to benefit the most from such a re-evaluation. Just don't mind the fact that I happen to belong to that demographic.

The idea that a person of color will be late to a given event is one of the most pervasive stereotypes in American culture. I myself have told Black and brown friends of mine that the start time for an event is thirty minutes earlier than it actually is, just so that they will arrive at a reasonable time. And I've been subjected to the same exact strategy by others. Lateness isn't unique to any one demographic, but no person of color could convincingly argue that we're not regular practitioners of it. We fully embrace this stereotype, and have even come up with a name for it: CPT, or "colored people time." If Elizabeth invites her friend Destiny to a brunch that starts at 1 P.M. EST, Destiny will arrive at 1 P.M. CPT, which, after time zone conversion, could be any-where from fifteen to sixty minutes late. It's a common occurrence, one that will be easier for Elizabeth to deal with the sooner she accepts it as a fact of life.

"Why are people of color so late to things?" a white friend of mine once asked me in college. Her sister recently had a child with a Black man whose Black friends were egregiously late to the baby shower.

I was a little taken aback by the question. *Why am I representing random Black people as if the state appointed me as their public defender?* "Your Honor, *Rush Hour 2* was on TNT for the third time that week, and my clients simply couldn't help themselves." Of course, I couldn't explain to my friend why this happened, broadly speaking, and I didn't care to.

I supposed there were a few good reasons to be late to things. Taking some extra time to get ready can alleviate the stress of feeling rushed, allowing you to arrive on the scene more relaxed and composed. Also, you get to skip the more awkward lags commonly experienced at the start of an event, with everyone desperate to find something to talk about before food and drinks do their trick. By the time you get there late, the lovely couple in the corner has already gone through the talking points of how they definitely don't regret having children, and now you can engage them at ease. Both these explanations are true, but they don't explain the stereotype about people of color.

There are certainly parts of the world that don't share the same dedication to punctuality that the Western world does. The country my parents came from, Eritrea, certainly doesn't. You would be a fool to show up for an Eritrean event less than an hour late. But alas, I could not use that excuse in American circles in Columbus, Ohio.

As unsavory as my friend's question was, she was far from the first person to wonder about this phenomenon. As Kat Chow, a founding member of the *Code Switch* team and podcast, wrote for NPR, one of the earliest mentions of "colored people's time" came from a 1914 issue of *The Chicago Defender*, in which a man named D. W. Johnson bemoaned the lack of punctuality in his community:

> If there is any fault among colored people that needs an immediate remedy, it is a lack of punctuality, to learn how necessary it is to be

on time, to be prompt and punctual in their engagements, to meet on time at social and public gatherings. It is perfectly absurd that so many of our people, sometimes unconsciously and sometimes willfully, wholly disregard the important fact of punctuality. . . . We have in our method of gathering what is commonly called, in the vernacular of the street, "colored people's time."

The amount of spinning D.W. must be doing in his grave today would humble Simone Biles. Despite his pleas, this problem, the way Johnson saw it, has only persisted. Not only that, but it is also embraced by the very people he critiqued. People of color have championed this stereotype, transitioning it from a mere insult to a source of amusement. And why shouldn't we? If there's anyone in this country who deserves to be late to brunch, it's me and, more broadly, other people of color. And it's not just that we deserve to be late, but our lateness should be allowed, accepted. Legislatively. Codified into the country's most revered texts.

Despite centuries of injustice and marginalization, the discourse around reparations for Black Americans is considered unwanted, at best. I therefore offer a modest, yet crucial proposal, one that won't ruffle the feathers of covertly racist Republicans who happily take subsidies from the government when it suits them, but who scowl at this same idea for Black people: We should be allowed to be late. Since the end of the Civil War, proposals on how to rectify the horrors of slavery have caused tempers to simmer and boil over time and time again. The infamous promise of "forty acres and a mule"—meant to redistribute land to formerly enslaved people to smooth the process of economic freedom and independence—like most promises made to the oppressed by the oppressor, never materialized. The idea of reparations was nipped in the bud.

Reparations may seem radical to those of us hundreds of years removed from the initial violations of enslavement, but they aren't abnormal. Germany paid reparations to Holocaust survivors. Some countries in South America have divvied out compensation to various groups who were ostracized by their governments. Even the United States paid settlements to Japanese American victims of its racist internment camps. But when it comes to the descendants of American slavery, the idea of reparations slides too easily into concerns about "handouts" and "reverse racism."

I don't imagine this country will be ready to genuinely consider a proposal of monetary reparations in my lifetime, so I offer an alternative form of justice that's much easier for Texas conservatives to swallow: a legal right for Black Americans and people of color to be late without social repercussions.

This could usher in a new era of allyship, a version of solidarity more useful than merely including "Black Lives Matter" in the bio section of your social media profile. In fact, restaurants and other businesses could throw away their sometimes well-intentioned but often performative BLACK LIVES MATTER signs and, instead, commission a CPT PROUDLY ACCEPTED HERE banner for their storefronts. Who among my white friends and colleagues will stand up for my right to be tardy anywhere and everywhere? To be clear, they already accept this about me, but will they support it as a matter of *policy*? I would be much happier to endure the steady onslaught of microaggressions at work if my employer allowed me to get there an hour after everyone else with no consequences. That job interview shouldn't start until I get there, and that flight shouldn't take off until I'm seated on the plane.

You may be thinking this is ridiculous. Surely, American society would crumble if people of color were granted a formal right to be late. You may be thinking that waiting for me to get to the bowling alley is a crime—but waiting is not the end of the world, my friend. In fact, waiting for me to get to brunch can be a small act of reparative patience, a moment of reflection on the historical inequities that have shaped Black lives. Or something like that. I'll even propose a template for this new law:

There shall be no penalty, social or otherwise, issued as a consequence of a person or persons being late to a given gathering for up to one (1) hour of tardiness, so long as they belong to the protected class of racial minorities. If the person or persons are of mixed race, then they shall be allotted such protection for up to thirty (30) minutes. Informal additions and expansions of this law shall be made without repercussions.

Since this country's inception, the gears that operate it have been oiled to favor white people specifically, and the result is that white people are much better established financially in the so-called American way of life than their Black and brown counterparts. Republicans love to pontificate about how minorities just need to "pick themselves up by their bootstraps," but this country gave its white citizens new boots at birth. Meanwhile, minorities had to exchange blood, sweat, and tears for used, patched-up boots whose soles were falling off—imagine the classic (and wildly offensive) depiction of homeless people in 1950s cartoons, polka-dot cloth bag on a stick and all—and they didn't acquire these boots until much later in life, and many of them had to buy them at a predatory price. Also, the boots were too small and had a hole in them that forced a single toe to stick out. And they smelled like the concrete floor in a moldy basement. Those boots slowed minorities down considerably, rendering them much less financially and socially stable than their white colleagues, friends, and neighbors. Some of the laws that enshrined this inequality have been repealed, but in my, at this point, tired analogy, this means only that the smelly old boot has been slightly repaired. A Band-Aid fix, so to speak. White people are still miles ahead on the path to glory.

Black and brown people can't ignore this fact. Why, then, should we be expected to perform punctually as easily as the people who have historically held us back? Being upset at us for our lateness is like being upset at LeBron James for failing to beat the 2018 Golden State Warriors (arguably the greatest basketball team ever assembled) when the rest of his team could be bested by a Division II college basketball squad. (See YouTube TV's promotional graphic that pits Steph Curry, Kevin Durant, and Klay Thompson against LeBron James, Tristan Thompson, and Kyle Korver.)

In a country and economy ruled by time, there are few better forms of reparations than letting me into an art gallery after it closed for the day. A federally permitted belatedness for people of color is the only way forward. The concept of punctuality has been used against us, and so we must be compensated accordingly: Black and brown kids should be allowed to be late to soccer practice. My dad should be allowed to be late to church (something he would never be, but he should be *allowed* to be). That flight should not be allowed to leave without him because of all the times he was subjected to "random" searches by the TSA. I want to be able to walk into Balthazar in SoHo at its busiest time and find a table allocated for a party of color who have made no effort to be there on time. Limited-time discounts at our country's biggest retail stores should be in effect longer for people of color. And I should be allowed to buy McDonald's Shamrock Shakes long after St. Patrick's Day, as well as all the half-off Valentine's Day candy well into the summer.

Minorities have often been victimized by expectations of punctuality. White society has kept its pristine boot (and bootstraps) on the neck of the oppressed, causing us to be late, only to then turn around and judge us for it. It's high time society lifted its boot from my neck, which is already strained from holding up a larger-than-average-size head, and dismissed the notion of punctuality. Only then can we truly be free.

D. W. Johnson would be dismayed to hear that by the 1970s, Black intellectuals were heralding CPT as a means of fighting back against the Man, but to be fair, they were on to something. In a 1972 issue of *Black World Magazine,* Ronald Walcott wrote that CPT was a type of societal protest:

CP Time is usually spoken of in tones of the profoundest dismay (by Blacks who lament their brothers' "irresponsibility that will hold us all back") or of outraged complacency (by whites who see this habitual lateness as yet further instance of our don't-give-a-damn-attitude, "but really, what can you expect?") or of amused tolerance (by the rest of us who are so accustomed to it we hardly notice it). CP Time actually is an example of Black people's effort to evade, frustrate and ridicule the value-reinforcing strictures of punctuality that so well serve this coldly impersonal technological society. Time is the very condition of Western civilization that oppresses so brutally.

I don't know if Walcott's argument is true—that CPT has always represented a protest—but I do know that until racial equity is achieved, communities of color should adopt lateness as gospel and codify it into law. Until the day comes that the average household of color earns as much as the average white household and, more important, holds as much net wealth, it is imperative for the government to protect my decision to be late as hell to the Regal Cinemas theater. In fact, the movie screening should not start until every person of color who purchased a ticket has arrived. (And every white person in attendance should be grateful I showed up before the movie started anyway, because I happen to love the *Mission: Impossible* franchise.)

I may be late to brunch, but racial equity and racial justice (by virtue of being nonexistent) are also running on colored people time. There is nothing tardier than justice. And until it gets here, why the hell should I ever be considerate of punctuality?

The Zulu warriors of Bravo Team were late to their battle at Isandlwana, but their army won anyway. The British were defeated for the time being, and the Zulu Nation lived to fight another day. Everything was fine until Bravo Team felt guilty about letting their comrades down. The next day, wanting to make up for the mistake, they marched on a British Army base and were all immediately killed. The harsh boundaries of punctuality, and the societal response to the pushing of such boundaries, had ruined yet more lives.

Bravo Team deserved better . . . but in a world where those of us who have been exploited by timeliness can now be empowered to be late, freedom exists. The mighty but tardy Zulu warriors were forced to operate on the timeline of the British invaders, and so they had their agency stripped from them. Time was not their enemy; it was simply being used against them. Nearly 150 years later, let us not suffer the same fate. Let me be late to brunch.

6

THE OCARINA
OF TIME

When I was ten years old, my dad tired of seeing me spend all my time gaming—which included an attempt to unlock Goku as a secret character on *Tony Hawk's Pro Skater 2*. Apparently, the *Dragon Ball Z* character could become playable if you performed an incredibly complex skate move correctly: a combination of buttons pressed in a precise order in three seconds or less while the pixelated alt-punk skater was airborne. Executing this move the right way felt impossible. I tried endlessly (probably for an hour) and started to feel like I was inching ever closer, but Goku was nowhere to be found. And he never would be found. His cameo was nothing more than a rumor spread across the country's elementary school grapevine. Deep down, I think I knew that my mission to unlock Goku was futile, but I still had to try.

My dad, who worked tirelessly at his shop, Fidel Auto Repair, could not have cared less about my determined pursuit. His version of time well spent was going to the library to pick out books to read. But I had more important matters to attend to, like trying to confirm whether Activision, a Santa Monica–based video game company, paid for the IP of a Japanese animation studio and then hid that investment under an incomprehensible gameplay mechanic.

Concerned by how much time I was wasting, my dad signed me up for a summer camp program run by our local community college in Columbus. Magnanimously, he broke this news on the morning the day camp started. I fussed at first, but when he told me that my cousin Abel was going too, I changed my tune. I was always trying to impress Abel and his older brothers, so I now viewed this camp as an exciting new opportunity to appear cool. I packed my stuff.

A couple of hours later, I found myself in the middle of a cafeteria with about fifty screaming gremlins. One of them ran around telling everyone we were going swimming later. I was excited because I had never gone swimming before. Central Ohio is landlocked, and my family wasn't the type to road-trip it to a beach (and I mean a proper beach, for the Ohioans reading this, not imported sand around a dam). I never had the need to learn to swim. My relationship with water at that point was limited to water balloon fights and that disgusting thing kids do where they soak a rag in water and then bite on the rag and suck the water out of it. Don't act like you've never done it.

Expecting to bear witness to a vast and beautiful water mass, we campers were loaded onto a school bus and driven to a glorified lake just outside of the city. But first, each of us had to choose a partner for the phoned-in water safety protocol. The idea was that whenever the lifeguard blew his whistle, you were supposed to grab your partner's hand and hold it up in the air for a head count, so the lifeguard could easily see if anyone was missing or in trouble. Abel was my partner because, who else would it be?

After this safety drill, all the kids rushed into the greenish water. I followed suit, just a tad behind Abel. But as I approached the water, my excitement began to wane. Something felt off. Everyone else looked like they were having fun, though. So, I jumped in.

And that was when I realized, at age ten, that human beings do not automatically float. I immediately began sinking, then flailing around, trying to grab on to anything, sometimes grasping Abel's arm before it would slip away. He recognized my distress and was trying to lift my head above the water's surface, but I was too panicked.

My body's refusal to come up for air came at the worst possible moment. Just then, the likely hungover lifeguard blew his damn whistle and began counting partners.

But Abel's pulling my arm up to help me breathe must have looked to the lifeguard like hands raised for the head count.

I sank a little deeper and inhaled a lot of water. From below, I could see the surface of the water and beyond, into the cloudless and sunny sky. Rays of light shone down past my scrawny little body and onto the algae and rocks below me. If it hadn't been for my desperate gasping and writhing, it would have been quite a relaxing scene.

When I glanced at the underbelly of the surface, it felt like a different dimension. The water wasn't necessarily clear, but I could make out rocks and dirt and little bugs bouncing in and out of the light piercing the surface. Things seemed to move more slowly here than they did on land, so every motion appeared more vivid. Contributing to the calm atmosphere was my own body, newly immobile. Then I blacked out.

The next thing I remember is lying on my back on the shore of the lake, and the lifeguard doing chest compressions on me, even though I was breathing. During the compressions, I looked around at a gathering of kids who came to see which loser needed rescuing from relatively shallow water.

"Um, I'm alive," I remember saying.

The lifeguard said, "Oh, shit."

How could water be so dangerous? The same water that cleaned me, the same water I sucked out of a rag for fun. It was a substance required for life, but it could also be destructive. Water nourishes the earth, but it can devastate in the form of floods, hurricanes, monsoons, and tsunamis that topple whole cities. Water can also drown a small boy.

To this day, if I stand in the shower a certain way, or splash my face with cold water, it triggers a traumatic response, the memory of me gasping for air in that lake. I'm not sure what other effects this near-drowning incident had on my health, but the body really does keep that score.

The mental and spiritual wounds of drowning are certainly fodder for pop culture. Near-drownings—perhaps because they're an easy way to give a character some adversity—are a common trope in film. In the tenth installment of the *Fast & Furious* series, the villain Dante Reyes, played by Jason Momoa (who in a different film franchise, it is not lost on me, plays a character who can breathe underwater), finds himself knocked off a highway in Rio de Janeiro by a giant runaway vault of money and rendered unconscious before plunging into the river below, where he is legally dead for two minutes before waking up. Later in the film, the stone-cold brute says the experience provided some kind of epiphany and "opened his mind," turning him into a newly flamboyant and zany villain. In *Cowboy Bebop: Knockin' on Heaven's Door,* a movie based on the smash-hit anime TV show, the protagonist, Spike, is shot and dropped from a moving sky-rail train into the ocean below. He is awakened by a shaman of sorts, who tells him that he let the flow of the ocean carry him away. Spike then ponders how easily he could have died, and why he didn't.

Like Spike, my brief fling with what felt like the depths of an ocean (but was probably like five feet of water) forced me to confront my mortality. In that moment, I thought I was going to die, but at ten years old, I evidently hadn't lived long enough to trigger that life-flashing-before-your-eyes phenomenon that so many people claim to experience. Instead, I just wished so badly to be out of the water. And I wanted my mom. The experience was so brutal and jolting that I wished I could teleport to the very near future, not caring whether I was saved or dead, just as long as I was no longer in the present. And because I ultimately lost consciousness, it did kind of feel like I hit the fast-forward button. I time-traveled just a few minutes into the future.

About a year later, the emotional shock of the event had all but gone, but I couldn't shake that desire to transcend the boundaries of time. I daydreamed about temporarily being zapped out of existence. In sports, a "time-out" is crucial. It literally stops the clock, freezing the game's momentum, allowing the coach and their players to reassess their situation and make a plan to adapt. Imagine if we had this ability in our regular, everyday life. After all, we didn't ask to be here. Yes, life is full of wonder and beauty, but a lot of that feels outnumbered by people, events, and ideas that are troubling and difficult to understand. And now there are eight billion people on the planet who must also reckon with life's chaos, noise, and pain through no choice of their own. It's pretty common, I suppose, to not want to be somewhere— like a dinner, or a party, or in the back of an Uber where the driver is fondly reminiscing about George W. Bush's presidency—but that feeling doesn't always stem from a life-or-death situation near the bottom of a brackish, unimpressive body of water in Ohio.

In that year after the incident, I came across a

years-old video game that offered me the chance to play through my desire to manipulate time. This wasn't just a plot point either, but an active gameplay mechanic—an expression of the rules and systems that determine how a player engages with the game. The game was Shigeru Miyamoto's groundbreaking, industry-shattering 1998 classic, *The Legend of Zelda: Ocarina of Time*. Many seemingly basic aspects of modern gaming—like the ability to "lock on" to enemies or the addition of context-sensitive inputs (basically, a single button that does different things based on the given situation)—were birthed by *Ocarina of Time*. The game also revolutionized video game storytelling by allowing the player to go back and forth between two moments in time, seven years apart.

Princess Zelda tasks the player, Link, with traversing time, setting off events that affect the future. Link, via the player, then uses clues from that future to solve puzzles in the past—all to prevent the rise of the evil warlock Ganondorf. Link is nine or ten years old in the "past" section of the game—the same age I was when I lost consciousness at the bottom of that lake. The plot of the game is quite confusing, but I was obsessed with the idea of being able to magically pull myself out of a moment, and I imagined what would happen if I had the ability to skip seven years like Link does.

If I could have summoned that power as I struggled in that water, I would have—pulling myself out of crisis and into the future, leaving behind only a few fleeting bubbles, the way old-timey cartoon characters who dash away will leave behind a puff of dust. Had I done that, everyone at the lake would have assumed I'd drowned. Abel would have told the lifeguard that the last thing he saw was me flailing for help. The lake, illuminated by the sun, would eventually have been illuminated by police lights at dusk. A dive team would have attempted a recovery mission, not a rescue one, but they wouldn't have found a body. Authorities might have drained the lake. It wasn't that big, after all. Still, no lifeless, bloated ten-year-old would have been found at the bottom. *What the hell happened to him? Was there foul play? Was he kidnapped? Did he run into the woods to start a new life?* The incident could have become one of the country's greatest mysteries, inspiring the creation of true crime books, documentaries, podcasts, movies even. The intrigue of the case would have plagued my family. Abel would not have been able to explain to people—nor comprehend himself—how I could have disappeared right in front of his eyes. My family would have had to bury an empty casket and live through the next seven years without that form of closure.

Meanwhile, and in an instant, the drowning child I was would have arrived seven years later, in the year 2009, as a teenager, in the exact spot from which he disappeared from that lake. This time, though, I would be tall enough to simply stand in the water. I would go to my house and come to understand that my older brother was off at college, but everyone else would be there. My parents would look the same, but I wouldn't recognize my two younger siblings, who would have gone through puberty, and they wouldn't recognize me, either. Not really. There would be a hint of something there, we'd suppose. Perhaps I was a previously unknown long-lost cousin. My parents, however, would know exactly who I was. They wouldn't be able to articulate it; they'd just know. They'd be stupefied. Where had I been all this time? Neither of them knowing that I hadn't been anywhere, really.

It would feel to me like the blink of an eye, but to my family, it would be seven excruciatingly long years. And like Princess Zelda at the end of *Ocarina of Time,* they had to go on with their lives without me. There'd been a gap in their affection toward me. The hole in their hearts couldn't be filled by this older version of me because they hadn't watched him grow. The unconditional love for their ten-year-old boy would have given way to grief, and rarely does grief get the chance to revert into actively unconditional love. I'd be my family's son and brother, but also a stranger.

BOY FOUND AFTER 7 YEARS would be the headline in local newspapers. Investigators would grill me about where I'd been and how I'd managed to get out of the lake without anyone seeing me. *How is there no one in the world who can account for where this boy has been all this time, including the boy himself?* Slowly, maybe over the course of a few years, the consensus would become that some kind of supernatural event occurred. Maybe a portal was opened. Maybe not magic, but science from the future. For most of the world, it would be a miracle. A boy almost died and instead was saved. For people who like to believe they're the smartest in the room, there'd be a huge deceit happening. Someone wasn't telling the full story.

In *Ocarina of Time,* Link's time-travels have a noble aim: to save the world. But in my hypothetical iteration, I time-travel merely to save my life and avoid trauma. I would probably consider this a net positive until I realized I'd have to spend the rest of my days avoiding media outlets, conspiracy theorists, and religious zealots, and trying to rebuild my relationships with my friends and family. The relief I felt from saving my skin by whipping myself into the future would be countered by the negative effect my disappearance would have on everyone who knew me. And considering how, as an adult, I can regret something as inconsequential as my order at a restaurant (before it even gets to my table), I know

I would regularly regret time-traveling, opening myself up to years of debilitating anxiety. I would think, *Maybe there's a chill afterlife I inadvertently avoided, where heaven is a dive bar that still sells a reasonably priced beer shot special* or *Maybe someone would have saved me anyway*—which is what actually happened. The deluge of hypotheticals, maybes, and what-ifs crash onto me, a blanket of uncertainty. Who knows? Maybe I'd save the world by time-traveling. Maybe my reappearance would command the interest and compassion of someone who would otherwise have grown up to be the instigator of World War III. The gears of war, though, don't move as fast as the gears turning in my head, powering an ever-extrapolating system of infinite possibilities.

Bong rip thought experiments aside, the drowning incident is kind of funny, considering that I confidently went into the water not knowing not only how to swim, but also that I even had to know how to swim. And this is the sentiment I lean on when I recount the events to my friends. Even now, I tell this story to draw laughter. How absurd is the notion of life, that one can exist and, just a few moments later, simply not exist? Even as I write this, there are an infinite number of ways I could perish. A plane could come tumbling down into Brooklyn—as one did in 1960, killing everyone on board and six people on the ground. A gas explosion in my apartment could turn me into a rotisserie hipster quicker than my brain could process what happened. I could have an aneurysm—like my high school friend's mom did when he was a kid. In one instant, gone. Knowing the myriad ways my life could end, I consider it a miracle I survived long enough for you to be reading this. Or maybe I didn't survive until you read this. Maybe I fell into an open manhole because instead of watching where I was walking, I was on my phone typing out an exhaustive defense of LeBron James's legacy to a random troll online. Endless possibilities that might never have occurred to me if not for my filling my lungs with whatever demented bacteria reside in that Ohio lake.

That experience has created an overthinker out of me, and accordingly, I think about my over-thinking a lot. How can't I? The fragility of life is already hard to comprehend, doubly by someone who has been close to death. It is understandable that the wanton nature of death should give someone the blues. You mean I can trip on my way downstairs to check the mail and die? I can go to the grocery store in search of honeydew and end up the victim of a mass shooting? Did you know that the human body can overdose on water, the same substance that is required for life?

It's upsetting, but it's not the only way to consider our mortality. At the risk of sounding like a greeting card, the fragility of being has helped me understand how important it is to be more present. The chances of our dying at any given time are constantly scrambling about, floating above our heads like the diamond above the poor bastard of a Sims character you designed in 2003. We supposedly have free will, but it's just as easy for us to meet the grim reaper as it is for that Sims character whose sadistic teenage overlord traps them in a pool with no ladder or forces them to operate a Murphy bed while in a bad mood, which leads to their being crushed. Rendered in goofy animation, these deaths are hilarious, but they're all the more reason Sims characters should cherish the moments they *aren't* being gobbled up by a vending machine.

In the *Cowboy Bebop* film, after Spike is ushered away from the ocean's grasp, he confesses, "I was really scared. I shook with fear. If one thing . . . if one atom had given way, then I would be gone."

The shaman who saves him responds vaguely, as shamans do, "This blue eye conceives all things conjoined. The past, the future, and the present. Everything flows and all is connected. This eye is not merely perceiving reality, it is touching truth."

Whatever you say, brother.

There is debate among fans as to how one should interpret the shaman, but I'm of the opinion that he's talking about the earth as a living entity. If I would have perished in that lake, so too would some part of the world.

Living in the moment—what a corny concept. I'm trying it all the time, though, and I've realized that it helps me find value in more things. A bad movie isn't just a bad movie anymore. It's the injector of a tiny bit of information into my brain that helps me grasp what I like and what I don't like. This doesn't move mountains in the depths of my psyche, but when you are acutely aware, as I am, that you could die before you finish reading this sentence, even moving a few grains of sand becomes meaningful. Our lives are special *because* they're fragile, not in spite of it. In the fourth grade, I almost *died* in a glorified lake, but as discouraging as that is, I should feel lucky. I also *survived* in a glorified lake. While I was drowning, my tiny lungs inhaled so much water that it caused me to black out due to the lack of oxygen to my brain. It was terrifying, but it's also miraculous that my brain did me the favor of shutting down some of my bodily functions so that the most basic ones could keep me alive a little longer. Our bodies, which are so feeble that they could burst if we fall off a bike, are also so quietly elegant and well designed. "What a piece of work is man," Shakespeare's Prince Hamlet says in a monologue. I know this because I was forced to memorize the quote in an English literature class in high school. "How noble in reason, how infinite in faculty."

Here's another quote: The German philosopher Friedrich Nietzsche (and also Kelly Clarkson) famously said, "What doesn't kill me makes me stronger." True, but I'd frame it a little differently. What doesn't kill you might make you stronger, but what it can and should do is make you a little less resentful that the steak you ordered didn't come out exactly as you like. What doesn't kill you should make you understand that the bank teller was probably having a rough day and isn't just a rude person. What doesn't kill you should help you realize that the bartender is probably not intentionally ignoring you, they're just overwhelmed. In a way, when handled correctly, "what doesn't kill you" should allow you to become kinder to other people and, more important, to yourself. A potential new outlook made possible by my awareness of both the preciousness and fragility of my existence.

Link, on his space-time-traversing trek to save the world, didn't have a chance to take in the beautiful and magical sights, or to savor the gentle hum of shoppers passing by in the town market, or to appreciate the craftsmanship of the walls surrounding Hyrule Castle. He was too busy taking to heart the concerns and struggles of the

Hylian people while trying to defeat the forces of evil.

And your life is way easier than his. I mean, probably.

You might be wondering if I ever learned how to swim. I didn't. Soon after the lake incident, I took a swimming class at a nearby YMCA, but witnessing my anxiety in the water, the instructors could see I wasn't ready. After that, I never bothered to try again. A little more than twenty years later, it remains true that if I fell into a pool deeper than six feet, I would die, unless someone was there to save me. I certainly plan on learning to swim at some point, to avoid that, but it isn't at the top of my mind. I do, though, now have a profound, almost religious respect for large bodies of water.

A couple of years ago, I found myself on a Montauk beach on a cold night, and I stood there in awe of the sheer force of the waves crashing into a nearby cliff. The violence of the water didn't prevent me from feeling I was witnessing something incredible. The waves slammed and receded over and over, a rhythm that mesmerized me. My heart rate skyrocketed, and I became overwhelmed. I was curious: How many pounds of force was I seeing? How in the world had mankind ever proliferated in the face of such enormous, untamed power? Suddenly, I felt like I was underwater, but without the physical commotion of that first time. I was being pulled here and there with vigor, but I was calmed by my acceptance of nature's dominion.

No need to pull Link's sword this time, I thought. *I'm staying right here.*

7

A LETTER
TO THE GUY
WHO ROBBED MY
GRADUATION PARTY
AT GUNPOINT

To whom it should concern,

I hope this letter finds you well. I woke up on graduation day feeling ambivalent about my success at school. I knew a lot of people who didn't finish high school, so I had already seen examples of life and found meaning beyond walking across the commencement stage. Besides, in my household, the act of graduating was more an expectation than an achievement. That said, still a great excuse to throw a party and invite friends and family over. Because my high school graduation lined up with my older brother's college graduation, we had a joint party, and the double celebration was momentous enough for family from all over the world to visit. An aunt from Italy. An uncle from Canada. Another aunt from England. And all their children. An unconscionable number of cousins. A joint graduation party thrown by a well-liked family in the Eritrean community of

Columbus, Ohio. In my eyes at the time, this was the Super Bowl of neighborhood celebrations.

In the days leading up to the festivities, my mom's friends—who were also my friends' moms came over to help cook for the big buffet that is a staple at every Eritrean graduation party. On the actual day, the same friends and moms arrived in traditional Eritrean dress. We danced, we ate, we laughed. There was a toast. Unlimited joy. Younger kids gathered around a then-ancient TV set to play *Super Smash Bros.* The older kids hung out in the backyard, more preoccupied with salacious, though low-stakes, gossip. The parents set themselves up in the basement, eating cake and drinking beer. People came and went throughout the day. Some came, went, and then came back. A bunch of friends from school who came loved seeing what celebrations in a different culture looked like. My dad walked around with his old reliable video camera from almost two decades prior—making the footage from my 2010 graduation party look like it was filmed in 1993. For hours and hours, we partied. We were celebrating being together more than we were celebrating a graduation.

But you were probably plotting at this point. The sun was going down. Maybe you were in an apartment somewhere or at one of the run-down bars around the corner. Or maybe you were at the bus stop or the grocery store. Seeing a movie. Paying a utility bill. The neighborhood was littered with dilapidated homes that were being used to make and sell drugs. Maybe you were on the porch of one of those.

"Junkies going in junkies going out / Made a hundred thou in my trap house." Gucci Mane rapped about these buildings back then, so I happened to romanticize them. I wonder if you were a fan of his. Nothing gives me high school nostalgia quite like listening to his 2009 track "Lemonade." Still a banger.

Anyway, you must have been in the area by the time partygoers started to come inside to avoid the mosquitoes. Maybe you drove past the house earlier in the day and saw it as an opportunity. As far as targets of theft go, high school and college kids have got to be easy marks. I don't say that to make you seem lazy or anything. It's just that if I had to rob someone, I too would choose a bunch

of dummies who weren't fully aware of their sur-
roundings, let alone their place in the world. I like
to think you were mulling over the decision to do
it, though. That's optimistic, but it makes me feel
a little better about human morality.

The sun was fully gone, and our front lawn
was illuminated only by a porch light and the tall
streetlights that turned on about an hour before
you arrived. The sound of cars with dirty engines
creeping up the road was normal on that block,
but this time, the volume of the engine's roar was
thinner. You and your motorcycle appeared out of
the night. Pistol in hand, you did your dark deed
and then took off.

You were probably miles away within minutes. Flying down West Broad Street, passing several Number 10 buses on your way. By that point
in the night, the traffic lights were barely changing. No one was on the road except for the few
wandering men who bounced from gas station to
gas station; and a sprinkling of prostitutes, one of
whom used to flash a single breast at me on my
walks home from school. All the reasons the west
side of Columbus, Ohio, was undesirable were the

same reasons that allowed you to coast down that road without the worry of being stopped. Maybe it was this environment that got us here in the first place. Both of us.

We were in the wake of a national financial crisis that rocked the households of several of my school friends. Everyone was going on about how they had to cancel vacations or how their parents had to refinance their mortgages, whatever that meant to me at the time. But the city had struggled before 2008 too. Over 1.5 million Ohioans were living below the federal poverty level, so many of them in Columbus. For a family of four, that meant making $22,050 per year. That's about $5,513 per person for the year, or $459 per person for the month. Consider rent, bills, living costs, and you're automatically operating at a loss. In debt, in public housing. Welfare programs. One point five million people who mostly meant well and were in search of financial security. Were you one of those people, or were you just selfish? Did you genuinely need the cash? Were you in trouble? Maybe you were the quite reasonable result of hundreds of years of oppression of Black people, which rendered people like us predisposed to poverty and hardship. The creative imaginations of an evil government over the course of U.S. history could have led us here. Did you rob us because you were impoverished, because you weren't able to make money, because you were struggling to find a job, because you didn't have good educational opportunities, because your school district was neglected because of racist segregation and redlining practices, which were implemented by people who did everything in their power to make sure they wouldn't have to so much as look at you? Or did you do it for the thrill?

While you were carrying out your plan, I was inside the kitchen talking to Mikey. Besides my siblings, he was the only other Eritrean at my high school that year. I can't remember what he was saying, but he was cracking me up. My older cousin from Michigan was washing some dishes when her husband came into the kitchen looking frazzled. He told Mikey and me to quiet down and go downstairs. Sure, it was the tail end of the party, but not so late that we needed to be quiet. What's going on? Eventually, I became aware that there had been a robbery, but even today, I can't remember how I learned this. Did someone tell me? Did I overhear it? I do remember how shaky everyone was. I vaguely remember my older brother quivering at the lip. It turns out he and a friend were the only ones outside at the time. It all felt like some kind of perverse lesson, experiencing this on the day I formally transitioned into adulthood. Mikey decided we should, in fact, quiet down. His cousin was the friend who was with my brother on the front lawn.

I can only imagine what you did to their psyche. A trivial conversation interrupted by the glint of your gun in the night. You stretched thirty seconds of time into an eternity. This might seem illogical, but I do think about how lucky you were too. My older brother is a gentle giant, but he could crush someone's skull if he wanted to. He was a varsity linebacker and went to the gym twice a day. He wouldn't hurt a fly, though, unless the fly threatened him with a gun and then briefly left itself vulnerable in some way. I don't know exactly what transpired during that robbery, but the fact that your chest wasn't caved in by an angry, balled-up fist tells me you never let your guard down. Nicely done. If my brother had seen an opportunity, you would have been on the local news at noon the next day. Instead, your gun froze him in time. You stole his congratulatory graduation cards, full of love, well wishes, and of course, money. You took his wallet too, credit cards and all. Then you were gone.

I often think about why I wasn't you. Not why I didn't turn out like you, but literally, why I was born as me and not as you or anyone else. We won't learn anything about that until we die, and we might not know then, either. In the meantime, I will inevitably wonder why I didn't turn out like you, at least. What are the pivotal events of my life that led me to where I was that night in 2010, and how exactly did they differ from the moments in your life that guided you to the other side of the incident that evening? At first, I wondered if the difference was solely in how we were raised. That seemed silly. Sure, I was born to parents who immigrated to this country and instilled in me sound morals and a strong work ethic and such, and I do believe that played an important role in what my second-grade D.A.R.E. instructor called "keeping us off the streets." But I also know plenty of people with that exact background in our community who fell into criminal trouble. I'll go even further: Plenty of folks with even more ethically sound backgrounds than mine, maybe from rich families with great support systems, *still* run into problems. So, really, what's the difference between me and you? I don't *think* I would ever rob anyone, but I guess I've never needed to. If it's not about how we were raised, then what is it about? The friends we made? Buildings we lived in? Relationships we had? Routes we took to work? Seemingly inconsequential elements of a life can pile up, I suppose, and that makes it hard for me to see you as solely a criminal. We are the result of a microcosm of microcosms, a series of tiny yet influential events. I can't know if you're better or worse than a criminal, but I know that by being alive, you're more than one. You're a son, maybe a brother, maybe a dad—which is so removed from the way our party experienced you. I wonder if you are even alive anymore.

A few weeks after the party, my brother got a

call from the police saying that they'd found his empty wallet in an alley. And that was the last we heard about you.

Just after you left, the remaining partygoers were a picture of despondency. The vibrant gathering transitioned into a scene of disbelief, sorrow. Still trying to connect the dots, I stood in a corner, disheartened. My parents, their faces painted with lament, began to quietly clean up the scattered remnants of the party. Half-empty cups of Pepsi and forks with cake still on them were strewn about. Friends and neighbors were equally quiet as they picked up the room. Some guests moved mechanically, sympathetic but surely wondering about their own kids' safety. Others gathered in small clusters, speaking in hushed tones, hinting at frustration. Hugs were exchanged, and people started to trickle out. A day of glee now overshadowed by the thousands of events that led you to your act of violence on us. But just as consequential was the resilience our house showed. Amid the sadness and anger, there was a glimmer of strength. My dad, always finding ways to offer a lesson, told us not to let this warp our perception of the neighborhood. I'm pretty sure I rolled my eyes, but years later, I knew he was right. The experience left an indelible mark on all of us, a stark reminder of the unpredictable nature of life, that anything can happen at any time. Who will rob or be robbed next? Whose night will be ruined? Whose life?

There's a weird thing that can happen in the wake of a dark moment. An hour or two later, I remember trying to make light of what you did.

"Enjoy that twelve dollars, bro," I cracked to some cousins. They chuckled respectfully, not sure if it was okay to laugh. Wherever you are, if you still even "are," I hope you found some kind of direction. And if you happen to be reading this, feel free to reach out.

Sincerely,
Manny Fidel

8
SUMMER
'16

The summer of 2016 is an island out on the horizon. It bathes in bronze sunlight, and waves never more than caress its shores. Here, natives celebrate life with a rhythm that is enviable to foreigners. Imagine laughter and the subtle scent of honeydew. By night, the air is filled with bouncy drums and warm lights. The islanders dance with each other without fear of how they are being perceived. Restorative and cathartic.

The summer of 2016 is an island, and it sits off the coast of a bustling mainland in decline. A city there buzzes with tension and uncertainty. Its shadow looms beyond its borders.

. . .

If you're a Black or brown Millennial, the summer of 2016 was apparently the best summer of your life. A mythical, if fleeting, season retroactively praised by an immeasurable number of tweets,

Facebook posts, and Instagram stories. This was before Meta and X, but the legend of that summer has survived every social media rebrand. Most pointedly, it will forever live on as a pinnacle of Black American Millennial culture. Born in the eighties and nineties, this group of people treats that summer like a highly rewatchable cult classic film, reliving it repeatedly and wanting to experience it again for the first time. To Black Americans of that age, the summer of 2016 delivered intense nostalgia long before such nostalgia was due. As I write this, it hasn't even been a decade.

In the years following the summer of 2016, there has been a desperate longing to "go back" to a happier, carefree time. Happiness doesn't belong solely to that summer, but among Millennials, there is no other period so collectively desired. The hotter months always consisted of trips to the beach, cookouts, and late-night outings with friends and lovers.

So, what magic did this specific summer conjure for us?

Back then, I was nine months into my first year of living in and around New York City. After graduating from The Ohio State University in 2014, I spent a year doing freelance video work in Columbus before realizing I needed to break away from the complacency easily developed in a city that is not small but not big, either. I was on the verge of packing up and moving to Los Angeles to do the whole get-an-entry-level-film-industry-job-and-then-work-your-way-up-from-there struggle that so many of my friends are still going through, but thanks to an internship I applied to on a whim, I landed in New York City instead. I could afford to live only in Jersey City, commuting to Manhattan for work every day, starting in August 2015. After nine months of barely making rent, I saw the dew on the grass begin to shimmer. Summer's arrival.

The most popular song then was Drake's "One Dance." The dancehall tune spent ten weeks at No. 1 on *Billboard*'s Hot 100 and went on to spend a total of thirty-six weeks on the chart. I do remember it being inescapable, but it is a slightly less ubiquitous hit that reminds me of "back then." In June 2016, Drake dropped "Controlla." In terms of performance, the song peaked at

No. 16, but according to many a group chat, it holds the top spot as the most-played tune for people who like to reminisce about that era.

For me, it remains the soundtrack to a particularly serene moment on a breezy bar patio.

The Black-owned lounge Ode to Babel had become a neighborhood staple, and that night, it took its rightful place as the center of the universe. It was the perfect amount of busy, populated just enough to produce stories to tell the next day, but not so tightly packed that it was hard to get drinks or make it to the bathroom. I chatted the night away with old friends and new, our faces immaculately lit by the bar's dim outdoor lighting. I was probably (drunkenly) pontificating about Brexit when the opening notes of "Controlla" played. Everyone looked as if they had just felt the first tremors of an earthquake. Every conversation became irrelevant, and before the initial lyric left the speakers, the entire bar erupted in elation. To be clear, Drake's voice isn't heard until the twenty-second mark, before which there is not much percussion to dance to, but we found a way to move together. This lack of a beat didn't matter. Our early grooves evolved into pure chaos.

About halfway through the song, its novelty that night started to wane for me, and I made my way inside to buy a drink. There, I found that the two bartenders who had so jovially served me all night were taking a break to jam. I wasn't even mad. Quite the opposite. Every single person in that bar, whether staff or patron, was caught up. The mood was euphoric.

Many of us didn't know that in the very near future we'd be longing for this time.

A 2019 study published in the *Proceedings of the National Academy of Sciences* found that dopamine, a chemical produced in your brain that, to simplify it for the sake of saving you from some jargon, makes you feel good, has a stronger effect when we listen to music we like. For example, although the song was released in January of that year, we were blessed with the longevity of Rihanna's "Work" well into the summer. Like "Controlla," "Work" is an escapist masterpiece. Both tracks teleport you to an island, but the island that "Work" takes you to isn't on Earth. The song sounds like it was re-corded on Jupiter's moon Ganymede, if Ganymede were colonized by Caribbean people. Rihanna sings many of the song's lyrics in Bajan Creole and Jamaican patois. Three of the song's collaborators—PartyNextDoor, Boi-1da, and Sevn Thomas—are Jamaican Canadian. I am neither Barbadian nor Jamaican nor from outer space, but I could have been when Rihanna's paragon of music bumped through the speakers of a club whose temperature was just a little too hot, in a good way.

One such example: a summer '16 night spent at Bed-Stuy's Lovers Rock.

Dancing can turn strangers into partners, acquaintances into friends, and if you both really like the song, it can make you feel like you've known each other for years—even if you're on a first date after traveling across state lines from Jersey City to Brooklyn. I always knew I'd eventually move to Brooklyn—Jersey City was cool and cheap, but all my friends lived in Brooklyn. While saving up for the inevitable move, I was happy to make the sometimes ninety-minute trek to Bushwick or Bed-Stuy to go out. One night, I

met up with a woman who was four years my se-
nior, which means nothing at all, but at that stage
of my vanilla dating life, it was just about the most
scandalous development. I won't use her real
name, but for the purposes of this tale, we'll call
her Rihanna.

Rihanna and I were never meant to end up at
Lovers Rock: The agreed-upon date was dessert
at a local pastry shop. We were both late (see the
title of this book), and the shop was closed, but we
could hear the buzz of Lovers Rock from a block
away and decided to check it out. The bar can
only be described as hot, in every meaning of
the word. The physical heat, presumably from
all the bodies filling the small space, hit me right
in the face, as if I touched its hair without asking.
The comically abundant exposed skin inside, with
a thin layer of sweat, glistened like freshly misted
fruit at a grocery store.

Even though it's only about the size of a two-
bedroom apartment, Lovers Rock takes ages to
walk through because of the sheer number of
bodies you have to pass around. Rihanna grabbed
my hand and slowly led me through the crowd to

the dance floor at the back of the bar. We politely shimmied as the DJ spun some Afrobeats that wouldn't find international fame for another year. When "Work" came through the bar's gigantic speakers, Rihanna must have noticed my face lighting up, because hers did too. We shared a knowing glance.

When I think of the ease of that moment and the rhythms of it, my own longing for that summer rushes forward, a Polaroid photo that just needed a shake for its image to emerge. Of course we couldn't know it at the time, but we caught lightning in a bottle of Casamigos tequila.

Around these joys, a weight would grow.

Being a person of color is inherently political, but after that summer, politics became increasingly hard to ignore. Donald Trump's bigoted path to the White House, alongside the galvanizing police killings of Alton Sterling and Philando Castile, created an atmosphere of intolerance and divisiveness grounded in beliefs that white privilege and systemic racism weren't real. This caused a righteous reaction in well-meaning but ignorant white liberals, who subsequently leaned heavily on their Black and brown counterparts for education. The process was good in its intent, but it meant that people of color would take on new roles in their friendship groups and provide new, unpaid labor in the workplace. Trump's 2016 election victory came with a surge in racial vitriol and xenophobia: the Muslim travel ban, the rhetoric around building a wall on the southern border, and the president's equivocation in condemning the white supremacist violence in Charlottesville, Virginia. For liberals, these affronts demanded "dialogue" and "active listening."

Over the next few years, things became only tenser, especially after the police murder of George Floyd in 2020 produced an even more potent wave of discourse on race. Black and brown people were again asked to represent and oversimplify the nuanced concerns of their demographic. Some of this wasn't intrinsically bad—I willingly participated. But it resulted in a new level of mental fatigue, especially for people of color still coming of age.

People of color not only found themselves having to explain social justice in the personal sphere, but they were also being asked to help make their workplaces more diverse. On the one hand, having a seat at the table could aid in the acquisition of agency. On the other hand, it was draining to continually have to recount personal experiences of discrimination, microaggressions, and inequities, especially in endeavors that ended up being largely performative in nature: I shudder to recall the long hours I spent in my job at a large journalism outlet cold-calling universities in an effort to widen our hiring pool, or doing exhaustive tallies of the people of color who appeared in our videos as both experts and talent—days' worth of "culture checks" designed to teach employees how not to offend and how to make sure they had the correct Black celebrity in a thumbnail image for an article about said celebrity. And in social settings, conversations about race became unavoidable. Friends and family members who had previously skirted around such topics now found themselves in deep, contentious exchanges.

It's no wonder Black Millennials longed for an earlier era, one admittedly still rife with injustice, but one that didn't necessarily require us to litigate it so publicly. Of course Millennial people of color would long for a summer we experienced before we were asked to publicly grapple with the weight of racism. Of course we would want to go back to listening to Rihanna without having to know who Stephen Miller was.

In the summer of 2016, Black and brown Millennials were not yet so burdened with the weight of our country's conscience as it dealt with bigotry on the front page of the news. To be sure, racism wasn't invented in 2016, but that was the year many of us were given the assignment of synthesizing it for people who had only just become attuned to the country's more nuanced expressions of hate.

In the World Happiness Report, a yearly survey produced by the United Nations, happiness is measured by "personal" and "external" factors. Personal factors include mental health, physical health, family experience, education, gender, and age—some of them circumstances we have little to no control over. The external factors include income, work, values and religion, and community and governance. I'm struck by that last one: governance. The report states that "governments set the institutional and policy framework in which individuals, businesses and governments themselves operate." What a government does can affect our happiness, and for Millennials of color, it's no surprise that the first Trump administration soured our outlook on life.

Again, it's hard to know who Stephen Miller is and remain a jolly person.

But the memory of the summer of 2016 helps. When I think back to all the best things that happened to me personally—like LeBron James winning the NBA Finals or my working as LeBron James's cameraman during an interview (yes, I'm noticing a trend)—I couldn't know how those joys would soon take a back seat to a new, cynical view of life brought about by not just a bolder brand of bigotry, but also the misguided liberal reaction to it.

When "Rihanna" and I parted ways at Lovers Rock, we were not headed home to lie in bed and ruminate on how to tackle discrimination at work the next morning. In fact, it was still early enough in the evening for me to meet up with some friends in Williamsburg. I met them playing pickup soccer. They were a mostly white bunch—as this country's "pay-to-play" soccer culture would have it, where excelling in the sport usually requires a decent amount of money to access various clubs and programs—and while their ideas about race were not as advanced as they would soon become, there was no expectation for me to be the group's arbiter of race relations. We talked about the Premier League and, if I recall correctly, our favorite cereals from childhood. Just a blissfully dumb conversation that didn't need to be productive or meaningful.

After 2016, scores of Black and brown people understandably concluded that it wasn't their job to educate white people about injustice, but that felt off to me. I wanted to help people get a better grasp on things, but I wasn't prepared for the toll it would take. I've faced racism my whole life, but it wasn't until the fall of 2016 that I was formally assigned to spell it out for others.

But in the summer of 2016, fewer white people were aware of the systemic racism undermining communities of color, and thus, Black Millennials weren't forced to hold their hands and walk them through it. The only thing I worried about in the summer of 2016 was whether the *busitos* driving around Jersey City would have enough space for me to ride to Journal Square in the hope that the PATH train would arrive on time to take me to Manhattan so I could then get on the L Train to Metropolitan Street in Williamsburg, Brooklyn, and then transfer to the G Train that would take me close enough to Bed-Stuy so I could make it to that pastry shop on time. My journey was in no way an emotional one. I did not have to ruminate as deeply on the ramifications of the wanton rhetoric of conservative politics.

In the summer of 2016, I was busy making my debut in a city that was still very new to me. I couldn't be fazed by what was to come, because it hadn't yet come. Back then, the Millennial of color was predisposed to being carefree and unbothered because no matter what, a warm breeze would brush their skin, a fruity drink would coat their tongue, and when the first twenty seconds of

"Controlla" played at a hyped-up bar, they would lose their minds.

On an island just off in the distance, there is bliss. We can see it out there, but it drifts farther and farther away.

9
MELANINTENDO

You were once a soldier, but you didn't represent a nation. Instead, you fought for a corporation unmatched in power and influence, one whose gigantic factories drain the planet's resources to produce electricity. You lived an extraordinary life while fighting for that corporation, dispatching monsters and patrolling the facilities. Traveling across the world, you imposed the militaristic will of your employer until, one day, you became disillusioned by the meaning of your work. You defected and struggled with your conscience. In this state, you were primed for recruitment into a radical cell of activists who believed that your former employer was a dangerous enemy of the environment and who thus worked to destroy many of its factories by detonating explosives inside them.

The world called them eco-terrorists, but you called them your friends.

One of these comrades physically towered over you and everyone else in the gang. His skin was dark and smooth, and he sported a beard under piercing eyes. He wore a dog tag on his chest, and most peculiarly, a rusted Gatling gun had been surgically grafted onto his right arm. A founding leader of the group, he had a burning passion for protecting the planet from harm. His name was Barret.

As you spent more time with this group, it became clear that your goal to right wrongs overlapped with their goal to protect the planet. Your journey together had a new destination: the city of Junon, where sources were saying something big was about to go down. In transit on an airship, everyone in the group locked eyes. Their silence was peppered with the sound of the flight staff's boots clanking across the metal hull. Barret, understanding the weight of this mission, slowly approached you. A tense air filled the room. After a beat, he couldn't hold his thoughts any longer. "We're goin' to Junon, boyeeee!!"

Maybe you kept playing, but here's where I pressed Pause on *Final Fantasy VII*. Did this guy who exists in a steampunk fantasy world just say *boyeeee* like Flavor Flav in the middle of a Public Enemy song in the nineties?

There I was, in my early teens, taken out of one of the most beloved video games of all time. This exchange happened late into the game's story, and sure, I had already been exposed to Barret's unique dialogue for hours and hours. Still, this one line stood out like a guy with a gun for an arm.

To be clear, gaming technology at the time couldn't support voice acting, which meant that every line of dialogue in *Final Fantasy VII* was presented in text form, leaving it up to the player to imagine what the characters sounded like. But there was no imagination required for the character of Barret Wallace, a gigantic Black man with, again, a gun for an arm. It would be tough to argue that Barret's dialogue wasn't written to make him sound stereotypically "Black." It made me feel like I was reading the screenplay for the satire slave drama TV show that exists in the universe of Issa Rae's *Insecure*.

"You look like you was havin' a nightmare,"

Barret tells the protagonist (and player), Cloud, who awakens after passing out due to a distressing mission. "But you gotta understand there ain't no gettin' offa this train we're on."

What accent was this?

At various points in the game, Barret's over-the-top dialogue becomes a parody of itself—like the multiple times he says "Shu'up" during the thirty-ish hours of gameplay. Who in the world pronounces "shut up" like that? (Save for some folks in the United Kingdom, whom the writers of *Final Fantasy VII* were clearly not trying to impersonate.) The writers seemed to have guessed how Black Americans spoke and decided to just drop some letters here and there.

It isn't surprising that a game made in the nineties doesn't do a great job at responsibly representing the many layers and varieties of Black speech. What is surprising, though, is that Barret's goofy speech is the result of the video game's English localization. In the original Japanese version, Barret is portrayed as more of a military jarhead than a 1970s Blaxploitation character. In a 2017 video by Kotaku, translation specialist Tim

Rogers compares the Japanese versions of Barret's lines with the English versions, and the results are baffling. At the beginning of the game, Cloud disappears after a key chemical plant is blown up. One team member named Biggs inquires, "Cloud . . . wonder if he was killed?" In the Japanese version, Barret says, "Ano yarou ga kanemo morawanee de inaku naru wake nee daro," which roughly translates to "That guy wouldn't disappear without getting his money first." This line tells us that Barret thinks Cloud is an opportunist. Instead of simply hearing "Is Cloud dead?" (as in the English version), Barret ponders whether Cloud ditched them. And because the game's low-polygonal graphics depict Barret with his arms crossed in this scene, one could argue that he's conflicted. After all, Cloud is the main reason the mission was successful, and Barret probably wants him alive, if not for sentimental reasons, then for practical ones: There are many, more difficult missions ahead for the gang. In the English version, however, all this nuance has been eliminated, as Barret's response to Biggs's question is reduced to, verbatim, "No way!!!"

In the following scene, if Cloud decides to talk to Barret, the Japanese iteration will say, "Kodomo ja neenda. Jitto shitero yo," which roughly translates to "You're not a kid, so act cool." In the English localization, however, Barret says, "Stop actin' like a damn kid. Si'down an' shu'up!" This translation robs Barret of his calm and paints him as a hotheaded and frustrated human being. It's almost as if Barret is upset that he's being misleadingly characterized.

The English reframing of Barret's dialogue is just one example of a historical tendency to portray Black people as aggressive and resentful. Whoever oversaw the English localization of his speech perfectly exemplifies implicit racism. This person projected racist characteristics onto a character who didn't originally have them. But perhaps more concerning is that this person had been *taught* that this is how Black people behave. Barret's offensive dialogue exists in the game because the person tasked with translating it into English thought that what they came up with was more natural than the way Barret is portrayed in Japanese. I wonder if the writers thought Barret would be more recognizable to the white, suburban American kids who would beg their parents to buy the game.

For most of my young life, Barret, the man with a gun for an arm, was one of the few fictional Black video game characters Black kids could look up to. It's not that Black children couldn't look up to people of different races—hi, Tom Cruise—but naturally, it helps if the role model shares some of your key characteristics. In a world starved for positive or even neutral portrayals of Black men, Barret was a decent option. He was a sound leader and a loving father of an orphaned girl, and he cared about the environment. But this only made it more difficult to understand why he communicated in such a reductive way—especially when my white peers had an abundance of role models to choose from.

At the time, there was a stark contrast between what I wanted to be like when I grew up and what pop culture told me I could be. My future was laid out in front of me: Would I become a lazy moocher, a one-dimensional source of comic relief, an aggressive thug? Naturally, the role models I had in real life weren't action heroes or mysterious cool guys in fantastical settings, the kind of fictional characters kids easily gravitate to. Yes, Barret talks like a barking dog turned into a man by a wizard's mischievous curse, but at least he cares about climate change.

Perhaps worse than not having great options for fictional role models was what the Black stereotypes implied about me to other people. If the world saw me as a threat in the making, why would they consider my youth? Black children are often the subject of "adultification"—meaning they're perceived as older and less innocent than they are and older and less innocent than white children. The founders of the Center for Policing Equity found that white kids are not expected to be fully responsible for their actions until their late twenties. "By contrast, Black children are often treated as adults by age 13, if not well before, regularly perceived as older, less innocent, and more threatening." The adultification of Black kids at its most trivial still presents itself in harmful ways. A Georgetown University report called "Girlhood Interrupted: The Erasure of Black Girls' Childhood" found that Black girls were more likely to be punished for subjective infractions in school like disobedience, disruptive behavior, and dress code violations than their white peers. And when taken to the extreme, adultification can kill. This is what happened to Tamir Rice, a twelve-year-old Black kid who was gunned down in Cleveland, Ohio, after police officers claimed they thought he was at least twenty years old. (I was twenty-two when Rice was murdered.) More recently, Kansas City teenager Ralph Yarl was shot twice after ringing the wrong doorbell in a case that researchers attribute to adultification as well.

The people who reductively translated Barret Wallace's lines from Japanese to English were complicit in the type of dehumanization Black and brown people have faced forever. Sure, they probably weren't thinking about how Barret's dialogue could make a Black kid in a low-income neighborhood in Ohio feel, but I'm hopeful that future generations of Black children will have an abundance of fictional role models to connect with. That was not the case at the turn of the twentieth century.

One of my favorite fighting game franchises, *Street Fighter,* features what is essentially a melting pot of the laziest stereotypes you can imagine. There are characters like Dhalsim, a sometimes emaciated Indian man who is always barefoot and wears shrunken skulls around his neck—his superpower is being able to stretch his arms and legs supernaturally far. Get it? Because of yoga. His fighting ground, or "stage," is a temple in India where elephants roam in the background. Because nothing exhibits the tranquility of an Indian temple quite like two literal street fighters beating themselves into a bloody pulp on its hallowed grounds.

Then there is Blanka. His plane crashed in the Amazon rainforest, which rendered him into a jungle-mad feral being who can no longer speak a language and must grunt to communicate.

There is also E. Honda, a Japanese sumo wrestler whose stage is a sauna. I applaud the Japanese game makers for this one, as they decided that they too should be subject to typecasting, what with the red kabuki paint scrawled over Honda's face and the references to the rising sun.

And for the United States, of course, there is Guile, a giant, ripped, blond tank of a man who wears army fatigues and whose stage is a military base. Hoorah!

And finally, there is Balrog, the only Black character in the early *Street Fighter* games, a skilled boxer who's all brute and is based largely on Mike Tyson.

Street Fighter's stereotypes are admittedly more fun than *Final Fantasy VII*'s Barret Wallace. They're offensive but not necessarily malicious. Every nationality seems to get ribbed, including the Japanese, the creators of the game. And crucially, *Street Fighter*'s cast doesn't have dozens of hours of dialogue to get through. This is a game whose makers wanted to feature fighters from across the world and who decided, in the early nineties, to make that fact *extremely* clear. Barret Wallace is more problematic.

Concerns about diversity in gaming became even more evident when gaming technology progressed to the point where players had the option to create their own characters. More modern games like *Mass Effect* feature hundreds of options for tailoring a character to look like you—unless, of course, you happen to (or want to) be Black. Until very recently, you could change your skin color to only a tan or a brown, whereas white players could select from a much wider range of shades. These same white players could also choose from long hair, short hair, buzzed hair, bangs, mohawks, mullets, bowl cuts, parts, spikes, and so on and so forth. If you were Black, though, you were lucky to choose between "Afro" and "shorter Afro."

In college, friends would come over to my apartment to look at the gaming characters I'd made and were puzzled at their appearance. "Manny, you don't have dreadlocks," they would say.

"I know, but it was between that and a shaved head."

It would take years and years for "triple-A" (read: giant-budget) games like *Cyberpunk* and *Starfield* to introduce more Black hairstyles, but I still found myself wishing for more options. My friend Kyle gets to give his character a pixie cut with a rattail, but my version of "variety" was being able to choose the circumference of an

Afro? In real life, Black hairstyles can include braids, dreads, twists, twist-outs, locks, high-fades, low-fades, high-top fades, curls, kinks, box braids, cornrows, lobs, shags, coils, ringlets, and many, many more. Playing dress-up is a formative experience for kids, whether it's in their older siblings' closet or in the character creation screen of a video game. As a boy, I felt left out of the joy of imagination, and I couldn't immerse myself in the games as fully as other kids. Just as with the lack of viable Black role models in media, it was the limitations placed on me that dispirited me the most. But before I dared to request a positive, nonstereotypical Black exemplar in video games, I first had to be able to imagine one. Was he a hero? A knight? A monk? In lieu of a real-life answer, I often did the work in my head.

What with the stereotypes of Blackness in gaming, and their limitations, I often felt dejected. Didn't I deserve the same quality of escapism my white peers received? Shouldn't I be able to envision myself as a character in a *Final Fantasy* game, one who wasn't a ticking time bomb with a gun for an arm? When I allowed myself to ponder who the perfect fictional role model could be, I kept returning to an unexpected adjective: *forgettable*.

If I had all the power, money, and clout to make a video game, one that would allow me to create what I never got to see in all my years of gaming, I would have it feature a Black person who was also the most boring human being of all time. A totally mundane specimen who would struggle to say anything remotely interesting, much less problematic, and who wouldn't have the conviction necessary to belt out things like "boyeeee!!" A painfully dull character would be the only way to even begin to compensate for the racist stereotypes that have existed in gaming thus far. Considering the zany and outlandish options from my childhood, I would have appreciated a character who was not comically taxing.

My new character, "Marcus," would be the protagonist of a video game called *Marcus Quest*. ("Marcus" would be his default name. As with many role-playing games, *Marcus Quest* would allow you to customize your character. When you were prompted with an on-screen keyboard, though, only the letters spelling "Marcus" would be available to you, but you could unlock more letters by either completing in-game challenges or paying me twenty dollars.)

Marcus is eighteen and from Village Town, a flat meadow sprinkled with a few houses and a farm area. The residents of Village Town often hear about epic tales and heroic feats happening far, far away—dragons being slain, beasts being bested, and treasures being enjoyed. Marcus thinks he could help, but the train out of Village Town simply loops around the surrounding hills and ends up back in the town center. The town recently developed a new track that goes farther into the east, but a storm damaged the station, which now must be fixed.

At the start of the narrative, Marcus is woken up by his mom, Marcusa, and his dad, Marcuso. Apparently, the mayor of Village Town has an urgent message to spread to the villagers. Once Marcus/a/o arrives at the town center, the mayor explains that monsters around the world are tired of losing to various heroes and have formed a monster caravan headed to more inconsequential villages. These monsters are in search of an ego boost, and Village Town is on the list of stops. Who will save them? The handful of villagers look at Marcus because he is the youngest villager and therefore the most qualified to fight. He doesn't have a giant sword that shoots balls of flames or a magical staff that emits dangerous lightning bolts. He doesn't have a gun for an arm. Instead, he wields a mildly sharpened pencil that carries enough bite to make his enemies exclaim "What the hell?" upon being struck. His armor is a worn graphic T-shirt that reads, DON'T TALK TO ME BEFORE I'VE HAD MY COFFEE. Marcus thinks it's funny, but the villagers think it's kind of embarrassing. Marcus's origin story is as thrilling as milk that isn't quite spoiled but definitely getting there. He has had no tragic losses, and ancient prophecies prohibit him from having a nice, calm life. He simply exists. In a world teeming with chosen ones and prodigies and destined knights, Marcus stands out by virtue of his sheer mediocrity. He likes junk food and going for walks around the village. He likes to read comics, and he has a crush on the girl who tends to the farm, but he will never act on it.

But now he has a chance to make something of his life.

The monsters have chosen a new people to bully, and Marcus is reluctantly forced into action. The villagers agree that it would be best to confront the monsters while they're en route to Village Town, which means they must fix the train station that was damaged by the storm.

Marcus's first quest: Help the villagers fix the train station.

He accepts.

Unfortunately, the bulk of this video game's playing time is spent fixing this train station. For about ten in-real-life hours, Marcus must retrieve wood and rocks from the surrounding hills, sometimes while dispatching foxes or goats that intimidate him.

Just as the train station is finished, the monsters arrive at Village Town. They burst through the fenced perimeter and stare down the villagers, their new prey. As they begin their approach, though, a beam of light pierces the clouds from above, and a figure can be seen floating inside the beam. Down comes a hero equipped with a sword and shield.

Oh, my god, it's The Legendary Swordsman!

The Legendary Swordsman is as white as his glowing armor. He holds his sword up to the sky, and a wave of holy light washes over Village Town, incinerating every monster that made the mistake of coming there. The villagers explode with joy and gather around him. He salutes the crowd—"Yeah, no problem"—and then blasts off into the sky, accidentally hitting a tree on the way up. The top half of the tree is ripped off, tumbles through the air, and lands on the newly fixed train station, destroying it. The villagers look on in awe, knowing what they must do—but it'll have to wait for *Marcus Quest 2*.

Marcus, the hero I think I would have created in my childhood, makes me think about which characters get to lack controversy. The villagers of Village Town can't adultify Marcus because I, the creator of that world, have excluded that concept from my game.

Thankfully, portrayals of Black video game

characters have inched away from infamy. Since 1997, the year *Final Fantasy VII* was released, Black characters in video games have progressed by leaps and bounds. *BioShock*'s Daisy Fitzroy is a smart, determined woman whose rags-to-revolution story manages to steer clear of stereotypes. *Halo*'s Sergeant Johnson is seemingly like the Japanese version of Barret: a highly trained military man with a "there is no try" spirit who gives humanity hope in the face of an alien invasion. And *Red Dead Redemption 2* features a Black outlaw named Lenny who manages to teach the main character about white privilege without sounding like a grade-school Black History Month homework assignment.

But when it comes to Barret Wallace, the progress has fallen flat. Nearly thirty years after the release of *Final Fantasy VII* came *Final Fantasy VII: Remake*—a perfect opportunity to reimagine the character into something at least half as off-putting. Yet, there Barret was again, a hulking Black man—except now with voice acting that sounds like an AI voice algorithm trained on old *Shaft* movies and clips of Mr. T. I don't blame the voice actor, though; he is of course being directed. The character whose dialogue plagued my previous playthroughs of *Final Fantasy VII* was back in action, except in much better graphical form and 4K high definition. With today's enhancements, Barret now looks like a real person, and some critics argue that the new version is much better than the old one. I can't quite square it that way. People claim that Barret has been given more narrative substance, which is true, but there's still something disconcerting about him. Despite this growth, he remains a bit of a buffoon, and he still leans into racial stereotypes—like being pissed off all the time and getting loud at the smallest inconvenience. In a weird way, I prefer the earlier version. At least the blocky graphics and text-only dialogue of the original game made the character feel silly. All these years after the original, the new Barret is still the epitome of the Angry Black Man.

Gaming, and media at large, is better off without characters like this. If the creators of *Final Fantasy* insist on portraying Barret this way, maybe he'd do well to switch places with Marcus in Village Town, an equally dumb experiment. He could work on the train station, yelling at people for welding the wrong way, and Marcus could be placed in the world of *Final Fantasy VII*.

Marcus, understanding the weight of his new mission, slowly approaches you. A tense air fills the room on the airship. After a beat, he can't hold his thoughts any longer. "Uh, it looks like we're going to Junon."

10
IN TIME

The land of Eritrea sits on the Horn of Africa like a crow perched on a power line. On a map, she appears to watch over the East, witnessing all that transpires, even the dawn of humanity. The earliest human remains found on Earth date back to over 230,000 years ago, the discovery made right there under Eritrea's watch. She presided over the rise and fall of legendary empires and kingdoms, societies and religions. She watched the region's natives depart her soil, trekking to different parts of the unknown world. In those newer places, the travelers' skin color changed, and they became different people, different races. This would eventually bring calamity.

Back on the Horn, though, Eritrea saw the caliphs of the Prophet Muhammad invade. She saw the Ottoman Empire claim sections of her land, followed in the late 1880s by the Italians. Persistent in her surveillance, she steadfastly remained present for every iteration of her liberation. After her people helped drive Italian militias away in re-peated offenses on her land, King Haile Selassie of Ethiopia annexed Eritrea, sparking a political and militant revolution by Eritreans who wanted independence. These Eritrean freedom fighters went on to endure a struggle that transcends re-ality, space, and time, as the task of defeating im-possible odds should, and they succeeded in their liberation from Ethiopia. But they lost an internal fight against temptation, forming a government that fell victim to the illusion of power through au-tocracy and became a cautionary tale and a blue-print for generational trauma. From time, it was the beginning of the end. But in time, it doesn't have to be.

It's been surreal to be Eritrean and watch the Western world fawn over former king of Ethiopia Haile Selassie. Conventionally, he's the stoic noble who victoriously resisted European devils, mod-ernized Ethiopia, and practically started a reli-gion with his 1966 visit to Jamaica, purportedly fulfilling a prophecy from civil rights hero Mar-cus Garvey. "Look to Africa when a black king shall be crowned," Garvey foretold, "for the day of deliverance is near." Rastafarians are named after Selassie's birth name, Tafari, and many of them believe Ras ("Prince") Tafari Makonnen to be the second coming. Bob Marley even wrote a song about him: "Selassie Is the Chapel." Selassie's official title was His Imperial Majesty Haile Selassie I, Conquering Lion of the Tribe of Judah, King of Kings and Elect of God—which makes it easy to see how the sheer weight of a name can enamor a populace.

In 1963, Selassie came to New York City to condemn resurfaced Italian aggression in the Horn of Africa, and in a famous speech to the United Nations, he called for world peace. Seven years later, he presided over a government and army that massacred entire Eritrean villages to quell the people's whispers of independence—a pan-African deity who slaughtered scores of Africans. In the end, he may have met a just fate: allegedly strangled in bed and buried in an unmarked grave in an unknown location while Eritrea pushed on with her fight for freedom.

As it turns out, though, Selassie's despotism was incredibly human.

The state of Eritrea gained official independence in 1993, formally recognized by the same United Nations that had welcomed Selassie years before—but it continues to struggle, its leaders succumbing to the same alluring power of tyranny as Selassie. Today's Eritrea is ruled by a man and a government that are guilty of their own atrocities: arbitrary killings, torture, mandatory and indefinite military service, and draconian restrictions on journalism, faith, and democracy. These dire conditions have caused hundreds of thousands of Eritreans to risk their lives to get to other parts of the world. The current president took power after Eritrea's independence was solidified, promising that constitutions and elections would come shortly thereafter. It's been thirty-four years— a year longer than I've been alive—and excuses for the failure of this to happen are parroted by the Eritrean government's greatest defenders, including millions of people in the diaspora abroad. In their view, the Western powers do not have Eritrea's best interests at heart. To be fair to them, it's hard to argue that the United States, for example, considers a "developing" country's best interests further than those interests could directly benefit the United States.

There is a lot to be said about bias when it comes to media coverage of Africa generally. As a member of "the media"—the amorphous and unhelpful umbrella term that describes pretty much anyone who's a journalist, no matter how unconnected they are—I have long critiqued the way African countries are portrayed to readers around the world. Reports about widespread famine or corruption or warfare in Africa too seldom shine a light on the foundational issues that led to such conditions—namely, the decades of European invasions that left behind a charred political environment. Much like how racial disparities in the United States can be traced back to the horrors of slavery, the fraught circumstances on the world's second largest continent are the direct result of the colonization of that continent—but you wouldn't necessarily know that if you relied only on mainstream Western media. These are the true circumstances that some in the Eritrean diaspora point to when confronted with the government's misdeeds. Still, for me, they don't absolve Eritrean president Isaias Afwerki and his ruthless regime of their crimes.

I spent much of my teenage and college years attempting to convince my Eritrean peers that Afwerki's government was a detriment to Eritreans everywhere. On my social media accounts, I shared activists' campaigns to get political prisoners out of jail. During the Arab Spring, a series of political uprisings in the Arab world in the 2010s, I wrote Facebook posts that criticized compatriots who seemed to understand the importance of opposing corrupt governments, but who somehow couldn't recognize that Eritrea was home to one of its own. The cognitive dissonance was almost impressive. I figured their pride and nationalism must have blinded them, preventing them from viewing the government in a critical way. I argued that it was entirely possible to be proud of your country while also acknowledging the missteps of its leaders. Still, my adolescent activism was devoid of a crucial layer of context: I had never been to Eritrea. And my detractors at the time rightfully reminded me of this. I was pontificating on a country I had never set foot in.

. . .

It took me and my older brother around thirty-six hours to get from Columbus, Ohio, to Asmara, Eritrea. For a long time, we have chalked up the length of that 2012 journey to a lack of available flights going there. Today, however, we're pretty sure the day-and-a-half voyage was the result of our parents telling the travel agent to make the trip as affordable as possible. This meant two separate eight-hour layovers, first in Washington, D.C., and then in Frankfurt, Germany. From Frankfurt, we took a plane down to Jeddah, Saudi Arabia, and then a smaller plane from Jeddah to Asmara. Nowadays, with the proliferation of Ethiopian Airlines—and if you aren't trying to be as frugal as possible—you can get from the eastern United States to Asmara in about sixteen hours.

When my brother and I first landed in Asmara, fatigue pummeled us into an exhausted Eritrean pulp. We arrived, quite delirious, in the nighttime and became newly acquainted with some first cousins inside the quaint, if not dated, airport. We linked up with our other two siblings and our mom, who had arrived a week before, and then went straight to the house we'd rented and fell into bed.

The following morning felt like a cultural reset. Before breakfast, I walked out of our rental home on the outskirts of the city and encountered a lone goat calmly walking across the nominal street. It clopped across the red dirt and then turned around, as if it knew I was staring, and produced an annoyed grunt. Just forty-eight hours before, I had been concerned about bit rates while converting .mov video files into .mp4 video files for my job at the state-of-the-art tech center at The Ohio State University, and now here I was in the homeland, thinking about how I might have to fight a goat. Thankfully, it never came to that. The goat concluded I wasn't worth the effort and continued to clop on down the road.

Later, we ventured into downtown Asmara, which looks a lot more like San Francisco or Los Angeles than the image that is probably in your head when you hear the word *Africa*—and if you have such an image, you should seriously adjust it. Apartment complexes and office buildings and monuments towered over me as taxis and scooters whizzed by. The bells of cathedrals and churches rang loudly. And the people! After growing up in Columbus, Ohio, for twenty-some years, I found it surreal to be in a city where everyone looked like me and my family. This place so far from home somehow felt comfortable. Still, perhaps because of our fuller faces and our fashion, it was easy for Asmarinos to spot us as Americans. Cafés and restaurants catered to visitors like us, but shop owners rightfully took advantage by overcharging us, before my mom stepped in to purchase the fruit or toiletries at their true price.

What struck me most about native Eritrean culture was the relationship the citizens had to time. You would be a fool to show up on time to a meeting, party, or dinner when Eritreans were running the show, and you'd be the only fool there for at least an hour. For people in the Eritrean diaspora like me, the idea that we (and East Africans more broadly) will arrive late to an event is as much a fact as the knowledge that five billion years from now, the sun will expand enough to swallow Earth. In the diaspora, Eritreans' lateness is mostly just fodder for lighthearted ribbing, but in the actual country, this lack of punctuality is embedded in the culture. Operating hours inscribed on the door of a quaint café in Asmara are essentially there for decoration. And as in other parts of the world, many businesses go on "siesta," closing for a couple of hours at midday so workers can go home, eat lunch, and nap. When I went to a church service in Asmara, people came and went as their spirits saw fit. Maybe this was how the Eritrean-Catholic Mass, held around the world, ended up being three to four hours long. It reminded me of TV before the streaming era, when shows would air regardless of whether you personally were in the room. It was up to you how much of a show you'd watch.

Asmara, in many ways, appeared to be fixed in time, a rare painting of the past. The Italian colonialism of the 1800s infused the capital city with architecture more suited to Tuscany; buildings with domed tops and pillars abounded. Most of the cars were old Italian models. People had phones but didn't seem to use them nearly as much as I did. Many residents seemed to hang out in cafés all day, an enviably retro lifestyle. But there's another, more sinister reason that Asmara appears like a snapshot of simpler times: The government dictates as much. During my trip, internet access was severely limited—I considered myself lucky to have successfully posted a single Facebook status—and electricity often faltered inadvertently or was shut off in planned blackouts said to conserve energy.

Much of the rest of the country is cut off from the world. In my grandmother's village of Tokombia, my siblings and I slept under a blanket of stars, the sheer quantity of which I'd never seen before (and haven't seen since). But it was hard to revel in this natural spectacle knowing that the government was deliberately sequestering its citizenry from the international community. President Afwerki asserted as much in a string of infamous interviews, declaring that the country didn't need help and didn't want to be dependent on other powers. It's a somewhat noble stance—until you grasp that, in 2019, according to the Institute for Security Studies Africa, nearly 40 percent of the Eritrean population lived in "extreme poverty."

The economic success of a given country does not necessitate leaving its doors open to the agendas of the world, but the poverty in Eritrea is a consequence more of government policy than of chance.

Independence, hard won and paid for with unimaginable sacrifice, was supposed to be Eritrea's ticket to a brighter future. Instead, the tale told of the nation is that liberators can, and often do, morph into oppressors. And although this is very tragically African, it's also relentlessly human. "Liberty, equality, fraternity!" screamed rosy-cheeked Frenchmen whose guillotine had yet more work to do after their revolution was realized. The Russian Bolsheviks overthrew tsars only to replace them with a system of cruelty that would have made the previous tyrants envious. It turns out that revolutions are expert at recognizing pain, but thus far have been lousy at addressing the structural flaws that enable such suffering in the first place. This isn't a condemnation—I believe that most revolutions are worth admiring—it's just an observation.

I don't think Eritrea's leaders set out to build a

dictatorship, but after valiantly leading their people to independence, they convinced themselves that they were the only ones who could continue its stewardship. Nationalism had united Eritreans against a common enemy for decades, but after that enemy was defeated, it transformed into a tool of control. How can Eritreans, and humanity at large, possibly break this cycle?

The answer is with time. The same resilience that carried people through decades of subjugation could one day dismantle the need for it. The Eritrean diaspora—the community that I have at many times been at political odds with—is the single most likely effector of change in the country. We can be a proud people and still shed light on the crimes being done in our name. In fact, I would argue that being proud of who we are *requires* this. Yes, the world has antagonized Eritrea and has even wagered bets, however unsuccessful, on its downfall. But that doesn't mean we have to placate the desires of its despot in chief. I can't help but look to the stars, the ones that blanketed the sky in Tokombia. What can humanity learn from us? All these millennia later, Eritrea is still the crow on the power line, and she deserves to stay up there.

The images I have in my head of Asmara, of the lowlands, and of the higher-altitude villages like Ira, where my father is from, are ones I—the longer I age and mature—would die to protect. And while I furiously oppose Eritrea's current government, I now better understand exactly what so many of that government's defenders are so fervent in wanting to preserve. Eritrea is, after all, a country that overcame impossible odds to exist in the first place. It makes sense that it remains steadfast in its mission to continue to prove the world wrong.

But those of us abroad do not have to face the societal repression and abuse that take place in Eritrea in the name of international autonomy. Instead, we visit every now and then, staying mostly in the capital city (which isn't so different from the cities we grew up in), rarely venturing out into the regions where poverty is most visible. From the comfort of what most people call the first world, we pontificate about whether Eritrea, as a state, is good or bad or developing or stuck. We fight and call one another names.

I can easily imagine supporters of Eritrea's government reading this and calling me a propagandist for some Western agenda. I vividly remember the emails and death threats, the side-eyes and the condemnations, I received both publicly and behind my back, from people I considered friends. When I meet older relatives who know I'm a journalist, they will tell me, in a playful tone but one that has a nugget of earnestness to it, how much the media lies and lies.

I also recall all the missteps I've taken. In 2009, the United Nations accused Eritrea of aiding and abetting Somali terrorists who were stifling peace in the region and voted to impose sanctions on the country. I remember logging on to Facebook and coming out in support of the sanctions. I was so opposed to the tyrants running the country that I couldn't process whom those sanctions would affect most: the people who were fleeing the country in droves. These days, I cut myself some slack: I was a teenager. Still, the experience taught me just how much of an obstacle rage can be in discourse.

I've been told that I don't actually love Eritrea, or that I'm not proud to be Eritrean, but just like for those who have said such things, it is my pride in Eritrea and my love for its people that have driven my sometimes-too-pointed rhetoric. Both sides of the vicious debate on Eritrea are united in our passion for its continued existence, and if we all took steps to formally acknowledge this, I believe the discourse surrounding its politics would be more effective. "I love America more than any other country in the world," legendary writer and civil rights activist James Baldwin once said, "and, exactly for this reason, I insist on the right to criticize her perpetually."

In my opinion, Eritrea is in dire straits. That doesn't mean that good things aren't happening there. Every now and then, I hear about a medical accomplishment, or about a student who invented a more efficient method of farming. The oppression and repression and suppression happening in Eritrea do not mean there aren't beautiful layers to the country, or that the people aren't warm and welcoming. They may be late to the function, but when they get there, you will feel comfort and hospitality that are wholesome and pure. This is a country that defied logic to be with us today, and as reprehensible as I find the arguments in favor of its government, I find the passion of its defenders to be more understandable in a way I couldn't when I was younger and more full of angst.

On a cold and misty morning in the village where my father was born, it began to rain. Despite the village's sitting toward the top of a mountain, it hadn't rained there in a long time. My siblings and I were packing up the car when the drizzle began to wet the soil, and one of the village elders made a comment in Tigrinya that prompted others to reach their hands up to the sky in a moment of praise. My uncle smirked. I asked him what the elders were saying, and he told me they believed it was finally raining because we American kids came home to find our roots. It took all my power not to shed tears in that moment.

We came to see Eritrea, and she cried for us. I like to believe they were tears of relief. It felt like she was watching us, watching this scene play out, ever the observer.

Long before she was known as Eritrea, the locals called her Medri Bahri, which roughly translates to "land of the sea," referring to the country's proximity to the Red Sea. As long as that sea is there, and as much as I can help her do so, Eritrea will continue her watch long into the future. Movements, militias, and leaders will come and go, but she'll remain, a witness to the rise and fall of even more kingdoms and empires, societies and innovations. In the future, someone writing about her will refer to this current turbulence in only a fleeting manner, on their way to some other point. This era will be a footnote in the story of something greater. In time.

∗ Acknowledgments ∗

This book—and, of course, my entire life—would not be possible if it weren't for my loving parents, Habtay and Bahgu. I thank them for sacrificing so much to risk their lives to come to America and prepare a more comfortable life for their kids. Speaking of their kids, I also want to thank my siblings, Merih, Metzlal, and Sammy, for being so supportive throughout this writing process and fielding so many of my requests for advice. It was our endless fun together as kids that shaped so many of the ideas in this project.

I am eternally grateful for my wife, Mia, who I would die for and who somehow loves me through all my flaws. We were visiting her home in London for the first time together when I signed the deal to write this book, and that is such a special memory for me. No one has been more excited about this book than Mia, and it was her energy that kept me motivated throughout the years. Mia is also a writer and editor herself, which was obviously a great perk while writing this book. I'll probably ask her to help edit this acknowledgments section.

I'm also thankful for my editor, Sun, who helped me evolve as a writer and who also helped develop some of the themes in this book. Thanks to her for helping me navigate the book life, and thank you to everyone at One World for believing in me and for your seemingly eternal patience for me and my many emails. I'd like to thank my literary agent, Tim, for seeing the original proposal through many of its iterations.

I want to express love for all my friends who were so happy to hear about this book at first and who've been asking about it ever since. In accordance with the title, I was egregiously late on delivering the manuscript for *Colored People Time,* but I'm so happy it's finally in your hands.

And finally, thank you to LeBron James.

∗ About the Author ∗

MANNY FIDEL is a writer and producer based in New York City. His writing and commentary have been published in *GQ, Business Insider,* MSNBC, *The Guardian,* and other outlets. He also co-hosts the award-winning *No Such Thing* podcast. He can be found on most social media platforms as @mannyfidel.

∗ About the Type ∗

This book was set in Mercury Text, a family of typefaces designed by Hoefler & Co. The font is available in a series of grades that have different degrees of darkness but share the same character widths.

ONE WORLD

We are a home for authors—novelists, essayists, memoirists, poets, journalists, thinkers, activists, and creative artists, all unconstrained by genre— who give us new language for understanding our past, present, and future.

Discover more One World books and sign up for our newsletter:

oneworldlit.com

Follow us:

 @oneworldbooks    @oneworldlit    @oneworldlit